I0160909

TEAR DOWN
THESE WALLS

Beyond Freeze Frame Thinking
and Name Brand Religion

HOLLIS L. GREEN, ThD, PhD

GlobalEdAdvance
Press

TEAR DOWN THESE WALLS:

Beyond Freeze Frame Thinking and Name Brand Religion

Copyright © 2013 by Hollis L. Green

      Library of Congress Control Number: 2013934375

      Green, Hollis L., 1933 –

      Tear Down These Walls:

      Beyond Freeze Frame Thinking and Name Brand Religion

      ISBN 978-1-935434-18-4

Subject Codes and Description: 1: SOC039000 Social Science: Sociology and Religion 2: REL077000 Religion: Faith 3: REL116000 Religious Intolerance, Persecution, and Conflict

Cover by Brian Lane Green

Author Photo by Carie Burchfield-Ofori: cariephoto@gmail.com

All rights reserved, including the right to reproduce this book or any part thereof in any form, except for inclusion of brief quotations in a review, without the written permission of the author and GlobalEdAdvancePRESS.

The Press does not have ownership of the contents of a book; this iis the author's work and the author owns the copyright. All theory, concepts, constructs, and perspectives are those of the author and not necessarily the Press. They are presented for open and free discussion of the issues involved. All comments and feedback should be directed to the Email: [comments4author@aol.com] and the comments will be forwarded to the author for response.

Published by

GlobalEd Advance Press

www.gea-books.com

DEDICATED

To my Colleagues at

OASIS UNIVERSITY

With gratitude for their efforts to build
A Community of Scholars and
Advance positive social change
Through O. A. S. I. S.
Institute of Higher Learning

Table of Contents

PROLOGUE

Tear Down These Walls

At the Brandenburg Gate, in the wall that separated East and West Germany, U. S. President Ronald Reagan challenged the Soviet leader to tear down the Berlin Wall as an indication of transparency, restructuring and freedom. The Gate was a limited passageway between a divided people and Reagan's call was for more than free access, it was for the breaking down of the conflict-ridden wall. He not only wanted free and unhindered passage through this gate, but also, the removal of the problematic wall that separated the people from family and the arts, music, literature, and the collective and intellectual culture of Germany.

Reagan was not the first to speak of tearing down a wall that divided people. St. Paul wrote that the partition wall of the temple, separating Jews and Gentiles, was dissolved by Christ's sacrifice (Ephesians 2:13-14). Mark recounted that the veil of the Temple divided from top to bottom at the death of Jesus. This opened access to the sacred and provided incentive for others to become participants. In the twenty-first century, there must be courage to tear down the walls that separate cultures and people from access to worship and a spiritual path. It is true that removal of the harmful aspects of walls will not bring impairment to the culture.

Open access to Seekers

Paul, a pristine sacred writer, was clear that the life and death of Jesus broke down the wall that separated Jews and the rest of the world. The walls of culture, language, or tradition should not keep individuals from seeking the Right

Path or route to God. John, the Revelator wrote *"the eternal gospel was preached to those who dwell on the earth, and to every race, and tribe, and language, and people"* (Revelation 14:6 EDNT). The walls that separate people and hinder free access to both public worship and private witness must be broken down, because the past sacrifice abolished the hostility and dissolved the partition between the sacred and the seekers. Since access is open to God's promises, all should become fellow citizens with the saints, and belong to the Household of Faith.

Early believers saw individual converts as building stones placed on the foundation of the Prophets that would become a completed spiritual building closely joined together and growing into a sacred temple in the Lord (Ephesians 2: 11-22 EDNT). What happened to that sacred temple made from the hard rock commitment of new believers? What happened to free access to spiritual truth unfiltered by human tradition and behavior passed down within a group or society?

People Joined Together

The place and act of worship has many names. This book uses the term "faith-based" instead of synagogue, church, mosque, or temple. The author does not use the word "church" to mean a place of public worship connected to a sectarian group. It is used as a broad term for people joined together to advance a moral or religious cause; that is, a community of faith, a congregation, a spiritual fellowship, a gathered group for religious activities, or any organization or group intentionally connected to a faith-based cause. Christian places of worship, Mosques or Jewish Synagogues are all faith-based and are part of the faith equation that has a moral and ethical obligation to influence individuals, families, and society through a message of grace. The term "faith-based" came into English use almost half a century ago to describe any group, organization or function based on religious beliefs or charitable intentions. All organizations loosely associated with a religious or moral cause are a part of the faith-based community. These are the people who could tear down the walls of misunderstanding, hatred, prejudice and racism that blocks the message of grace from reaching the world. This book is for those who desire monotheistic unity and see the value in a unified effort to change the world.

*1. Therefore, the prisoner in the Lord, implore you to behave worthy of the mission to which you are called, 2. with humility and gentleness, patiently and lovingly bear with one another; 3. giving diligence to maintain the unity of the Spirit in the alliance of peace. 4. **You are a single body with one Spirit, just as there is one hope in your calling; 5. one Lord, one faith, one baptism, 6. there is but one God and Father of all, who is over all and works through all, and lives in you all.** (Ephesians 4:1-16 EDNT)*

A Way Forward

All true believers must work diligently to communicate the message of grace in terms easily understood by the next generation. Someone must weaken the cultural walls that limit access to the Right Path and give individuals a way forward. Who has the audacity to begin the process? Who will unlock the gates as a first step to full access? Who will take the hammer of courage and the chisel of truth and begin opening the walls that separate people of faith in order to construct a better world? God desires all to find the Right Path.

Faith will find a way into the heart and life of those who hear the message of grace and desire to live a moral and ethical life and assure a well-spoken eulogy at the end of life. *For you were called to give kind words to others and come to a well-spoken eulogy at the end.* (1 Peter 3:9

EDNT) True believers have a call to share their faith and have an acclaimed tribute at the end. *The Lord is not slow concerning His promise as some count slowness; but is longsuffering to all, not wishing any to perish, but desiring all to take the way of repentance.* (2 Peter 3:9 EDNT)

One Path to the Gates of Heaven

Cooperation leads to friendship and friendship generates fellowship and fellowship produces solidarity of purpose. Social and cultural differences will always exist in faith-based groups. Being "right" is not sufficient might to tear down the walls and bring redemption to the world; rather, it is pointing to the simplicity and power of faith and the need to emphasize common tenets that bring people together.   The faith-based way of life should be a force to unite rather than a wall to divide. Those in authority should not permit the human factor or cultural limitation to complicate the universal values of the faith-based agenda. All must seek to follow the one Right Path to the gates of heaven. To do this, all must behave worthy of the unifying mission.

Synergetic Course of Action

All major monotheistic religions have elements of syncretism in their beliefs or history, yet adherents fail to admit this fact. The combining of different, often contradictory beliefs, becomes a major problem for faith-based people. To admit this religious syncretism would be to betray the purity of their present belief system. Followers do not see or do not want to know the facts about such blending of other beliefs and unrelated traditions.   This happens when multiple religions exist in the same culture or a new religion is force on a population. Normally, this does not entirely succeed and the former beliefs and old practices continue. Syncretism is the opposite of a synergetic course of action this book advocates. Syncretism is a silent or almost unnoticed step in accepting foreign ideas while the synergetic process is a transparent strategy toward cooperation in a common cause.

Personal Action can make a Difference

For years Dennis Prager, a religious Jew, has actively promoted an "ethical monotheism" as part of an effort to increase cooperation among monotheists. Currently, Dr. Ben Carson, a pediatric brain surgeon at Johns Hopkins University, was able to connect a "spiritual message" to bipartisan efforts to bring practical solutions to avoid the path that brought "moral decay" to the Roman Empire. Carson's common sense approach was a warm breeze in the coldness of American secularism. The recent Pope Benedict XVI battled against religous persecution and state imposed "practical atheism" and his words continue to reverberate around the world to unmask the secular forces that impose radical political and cultural secularism on religion. (Source: NEWSMAX 4/13)

Synergetic cooperation is not to suggest that Judaism, Christianity, or Islam should make a fatal compromise of their religious integrity. Culture and tradition are social glue that holds religions together. Yet, compromise ("*together-promise*") agreement is a necessary part of the process. A lack of willingness to cooperate and work together among monotheistic believers is a major difficulty in building a unified force to bring civility and redemption to the population of the earth and restore unity within the message of grace. Individual believers are a powerful force in this effort. Where organized religions cannot or will not function, personal lifestyle can make a difference and break down some of the barriers to personal cooperation in a global agenda that could strengthen the One Lord-One Faith message.

Hollis L. Green, Th.D., Ph.D.
Evergreen Cottage, 37321
www.gea-books.com

Quotations are from *The EVERGREEN Devotional New Testament (Complete Edition - 2013)* the result of a 42-year project to translate NT Greek into a common devotional language. Order ISBN 978-1-935434-28-3 from www.gea-books.com or anywhere good books are sold.

CHAPTER ONE

TERMINATE NAME BRAND RELIGION

God is not dead! Religion did not fade away as an old soldier. The predictions concerning the early demise of religion were premature. Friedrich Nietzsche's 1882 calculation about the early decline in religious faith was wrong. Both Bernard Shaw and H. G. Wells predicted an end to what they called the "religious phase" of history; they were wrong. Even as late as mid-century, Julian Huxley wrote about "God's last fading smile" and compared it to the grin of a Cheshire cat. None of these secular prophets was correct. Although attendance at religious meetings has declined, a basic belief in God remains deep in the human psychic. What is lacking is the dynamic faith that makes life a shared journey with God. Missing is a genuine togetherness and moral agreement in the faith-based community that creates a common agenda for advancement.

A Common Agenda

One religion will never produce world peace, feed the children or care for the sick and dying. One group cannot eliminate poverty, violence, drugs, human trafficking or complete global moral change. There must be a common agenda to make people moral citizens of the world before they can become mystical citizens of heaven. Synergetic cooperation is not to suggest a least common denominator religion or that Judaism, Christianity or Islam should lose their culture or compromise the sacred reality. Culture and tradition are social glue that holds religions together. This cultural bonding is strong, but compromise

(a "together-promise" agreement) is a necessary part of the
way forward that leaves no one behind. Where organized
groups choose not to function, personal action can make
a difference and break down some of the barriers to an
action agenda that could strengthen the One Lord-One Faith
message. Perhaps, a better missionary "second front" in the
global spiritual battle or a strategic "guerilla warfare" effort
could make a difference. Remember, the goal for a global
outreach is not domination or control, but emancipation
from poverty and violence and liberty to choose a personal
and eternal destiny in the hands of Providence. For this to
happen, removal of the barriers to personal faith and action
is required.

Second Front and Guerilla Warfare

A generic least common denominator religion is not
the answer, there must a re-energized approach to faith-
based operations on three fronts: fervent local worship
groups, eager "second front" outreach units, and strategic
"guerilla warfare" activity behind the lines to teach the
teachable and reach the reachable. No one religion has
been able to reach all the population of the world. All the
monotheistic religions have divisions that limit their global
effectiveness. Each group behaves as if they have found the
"Holy Grail" and have exclusive access to the "secrets" of
eternal redemption.

Little Common Ground

Tragically, there is little common ground; however,
moral leadership must start somewhere and seek to make
a difference in the world. Provided there is adjustment in
the hostility and rivalry, opening of the gates in the dividing
walls, and a self-evident common cause becomes a reality,
there is hope for a moral and faith-based agenda that can
change the world one person at a time. This common
ground must be faith-based and known to be true without

ecclesiastical validation. Moral lifestyle and personal expressions of faith are essential to this process.

Monotheistic Divisions

Differences divide and camouflage commonalities that could bring unity of effort in overcoming global problems and fulfilling basic human needs. The concern for food, shelter, safety of family, and world peace should be the common goal of all who claim to honor and worship **the one and only God, Creator and Sustainer of the Universe.** Regardless of the term used to identify the Supreme Deity: Allah, Jehovah, Christ, or any other acknowledged surrogate spokesperson: such as, Moses, The Prophet, or writers of inspired words. It becomes self-evident that all who serve one God should be working together to provide for the necessities and nourishment of all His creation. This would require finding common ground and advancing a common cause for the benefit of all of the People of God: this would restore meaning to "One Lord-One Faith" in the world. Since this is what God requires and the sacred founders of monotheistic faith requested, the human element should not permit organized religion to hinder this righteous cause.

Viable Faith-based Worship

The only hope for a viable monotheistic, faith-based worship and witness is an internal redirection of the heart and soul that brings with it a moral lifestyle and personal protest against the immorality of society. Such redirection will bring both a commitment to the cardinal tenets of sacred writings and a spirit of cooperation and teamwork among people. This change in the standard "religious rhetoric" could break the barriers of "freeze framed thinking," and "name brand religion" and make One Lord and One Faith meaningful again.

According to Sacred Writings

The words of David: *Behold, how good and pleasant it is when brothers dwell in unity! (Psalms 133:1);*

The words of Jesus: *"A kingdom divided is brought to destruction; and a house divided falls."* (Luke 11:17 EDNT);

The words of the Quran: *Let there arise out of you one community, inviting to all that is good, enjoining what is right, and forbidding what is wrong: those will be prosperous. Be not like those who are divided amongst themselves and fall into disputations after receiving clear signs: for them is a dreadful penalty. (Qur'an 3:105)*

The Line of Attack

Divide and conquer is the line of attack Satan uses against the monotheistic faith! This tactical maneuver efficiently deals with multiple opponents. It is a process to define one religion by detailing the difference from the others. Since differences divide and weakens the cause, Satan wins the battle for the heart and soul of the human race. How long will religious leaders permit Satan to control the "words and weapons" of the spiritual battlefield? How long will the monotheistic faiths permit division to weaken their stand against evil? The immoral lifestyle and witness of weak followers garbles the message of grace. Who will stop this mumbled message of anger? Surely, the "One God" teaching is sufficient common ground on which all monotheistic faiths can stand. The human element should not divide God's work in the world.

Differences Divide

Christianity honors Christ but divides the message between Catholic and Protestant. Protestantism has more than 300 divisions with multiple differences in doctrine. The central disagreements dishonor Christ and the early spiritual leadership. Peter, considered the first leader of the

Way, wrote a general letter to scattered believers suffering from religious persecution and emphasized that Messiah-like behavior was needed to correct the inferior aspects of a community before a superior foundation of faith could be constructed that would unify the message of grace in the world. The words of Peter speak to the central construct of faith:

> 8. *Finally, you must think the same thoughts, share difficulties with one another, having automatic interdependence with brotherly kindness; be tender-hearted and humble-minded: 9. you must not repay injury with injury, or hard words with hard words, but bless those who curse you. For you were called to give kind words to others and come to a well-spoken eulogy at the end. 10. For the one wishing to love life and see prosperous days; let him avoid an evil tongue and cunning words. 11. Habitually avoid evil, and do good things; let him seek and follow peace. 12. Because the eyes of the Lord watch over the righteous, and His ears listen to their payers: but the Lord looks directly into the eyes of wrongdoers. (1 Peter 3:8-12 EDNT)*

Judaism honors Jehovah but is a diverse religion and members hold a variety of beliefs and interpretations of Jewish law and practice. Three main divisions exist: Orthodox, Conservative, and Reform. Yet, Jews share a common core of beliefs and feel at home in any Synagogue around the world. The Book of Chronicles provides a brief Hebrew history and contains a primary challenge to penitence and restoration of spiritual foundations:

> *If my people, which are called by my name, shall humble themselves, and pray, and seek my face, and turn from their wicked ways; then will I hear from heaven, and will forgive their sin, and will heal their land. (2 Chronicles 7:14)*

Islam honors Allah but has partitions that divide the people who submit to God. The largest divisions are the Sunnis and Shi'ites. Sunni Islam is the dominant sect worldwide. Shiite Islam is the dominant sect in Iran and the surrounding area. A third division is Ibadi Islam the dominant sect in Oman. There are others in spite of The Prophets admonition to avoid division:

> And hold fast, all together, by the rope which Allah (stretches out for you), and be not divided among yourselves; and remember with gratitude Allah's favour on you; for ye were enemies and He joined your hearts in love, so that by His Grace, ye became brethren; and ye were on the brink of the pit of Fire, and He saved you from it. Thus doth Allah make His Signs clear to you: That ye may be guided? (Qur'an 3:103)

A Common Agenda

One group alone cannot eliminate poverty, violence, human and drug trafficking or complete the task of global spiritual change. Before a common agenda can be established there must first be an effort to make people moral citizens of the community before they can become mystical citizens of heaven. The goal for global spiritual outreach must not be domination or control, but emancipation from poverty, violence, and personal liberty to choose a way of life and an eternal destiny. Taking away the barriers to personal expressions of faith is necessary before removing the walls of division among faith-based groups.

A Local Experience

The purpose statement of a local Texas congregation was "...to win the world for Jesus." Since this was a dream without an agenda, they realized it could not be an effective global strategy, so they narrowed the purpose statement "...to win Texas for Jesus." Then changed "...to win Dallas for Jesus." Finally, they came to understand they were not even winning all the children of faithful members and even some of the Deacon's children were not believers. This clarified that it would take the combined efforts of many committed believers to knock a dent in the walls of an immoral society and prepare people for redemption. The Texas congregation finally changed their purpose statement to read, "The purpose is to teach the teachable and win the winnable." Since one faith-based group cannot win everyone, there must be concern for those left behind and enlist the cooperation of others to assist in the global effort.   Concern for the community must precede the effort to win converts; therefore, cooperation with others is a way forward.

The Concept of Ecumenicity

This book does not endorse the ecumenical movement because it is limited to Christian denominations. Ecumenicity should be a grassroots movement stripped of politics and sectarianism and guided with individuals who honor the power of a spiritual conversion that regenerates immoral beings into honest and law abiding citizens. This moral lifestyle witness is the only change agent capable of creating a vehicle through which large numbers come together to solve problems and create the better angels of ecumenicity. This suggests a kind of spiritual math and the multiplication of effort.

Spiritual Arithmetic

The wise man Solomon understood spiritual arithmetic and wrote, *Two are better than one because they have a good reward for their labor.* (Ecclesiastes 4:9-12) Moses, according to both the Hebrew Bible and the Qur'an, was a religious leader, lawgiver and prophet, recognized as the author of the Torah. Deep in these ancient words are the laws concerning obedience and spiritual arithmetic:

Then I will give peace in the land, and you shall lie down and none shall make you afraid:... and five of you shall chase an hundred, and an hundred of you shall put ten thousand to flight: (Leviticus 26:1-12)

In the Book of Judges (7:1-28) there is a record of Gideon, who reduced his large band of warriors to a troupe of 300, and gained full victory over a great army. Spiritual calculation is based on sincere commitment, a "few good men" with divine guidance could do what the masses fail to do with their ready-made programs. Obviously, little progress is evident since the introduction of ecumenicity in 1840. The self-evident limitations are clear: a form of godliness without divine authority exists within a restrictive sectarian framework that appears to deny even the founding principles. When individuals refuse to walk on the foundation stones that mark the Right Path there is little benefit for the human race. The omission of some monotheistic faith-based groups further complicates a workable agenda for positive change.

Muffled Religion in a Franchised Box

Is the character and social fabric of a multicultural society so complicated that a global faith-based initiative cannot work in the twenty-first century? Has foreign immigration opened the floodgates for pluralism and stifled the possibility of unity among faith-based groups? Is there no common ground on which to construct a global unity agenda? Does not all claim to serve the same Deity: **the one and only God, Creator and Sustainer of the Universe**? The ancient world of the Bible was multicultural, yet, believers flourished through personal faith and sincere fellowship with others. Evidence exists that faith-based initiatives could work in a multicultural society with small changes in both the attitude and the action of individuals who control various groups. Many individuals are practicing their faith effectively through witnessing and some local places of worship are alive and growing. Sadly, the institutionalization of religion has muffled the true witness and placed local congregations in a franchised box. This is not true of all faith-based groups, but the required franchise authorization should be a warning to all others. Since some faith-based groups can break the barriers and share the message of grace with their community, why not others? Why does the stained glass barrier exist? What is the inferior operation that weakens the faith-based witness? Why cannot someone construct a superior operation that works? To break the cultural barriers and reach a multicultural global society, faith-based groups must:

- Terminate Name Brand Religion
- Overcome Harmful Cultural Practices
- Reduce Cultural Distractions
- Remove Behavioral Stumbling Blocks
- Demolish Polytheistic Traditions
- Defrost Freeze Frame Thinking
- Diminish Top Down Programming
- Resist Governmental Control
- Decrease Dependency on Buildings
- Disassemble Local Outreach Agenda
- Abandon the Giant Paradigm
- Debunk the Melting Pot Theory
- Stop Camouflaging Decline
- Discontinue Family Values Chatter
- Eliminate Old Cooking Recipes
- Remove Symbolic Barriers

Flaw that Divides the Faith-based Community

A tragic flaw that divides the faith-based community is dissimilarity and this difference presents a misleading message. Common ground has not been emphasized nor a common faith-based agenda developed. Sadly, this is done as if the process of stating distinctive differences were an asset. In reality it is a drawback to the public understanding of the faith-based community and a liability to individual and institutional cooperation in areas where there should be a common agenda. This produces disunity, dissension and disagreement and points the way to conflict, neglect, and abuse of opportunities. It is clear that opportunity equals obligation. Any failure to first provide for the needs of a community closes the door to positive change outcomes. Such a dysfunctional system in the name of faith is spiritual abuse of the first order and contributes to the walls that divide a community. True faith and spiritual commitment will work to demolish walls and provide a simple path to faith that can move mountains of opposition.

Complex and Confusing Relationships

Most faith-based groups have not transmitted adequate experiential knowledge through moral behavior to succeeding generations to make genuine converts. This, coupled with the mobility of a multicultural society, has produced complex and confusing relationships within faith-based congregations. Consequently, religious practitioners, without intent, hinder the conversion of the next generation to a faith-based lifestyle. To make sacred worship viable in the lives of the next generation, there must be an internal redirection of the human spirit with less stress on sectarianism and parochial adherence to a particular dogma and greater emphasis on personal moral behavior and lifestyle.

A Logical Sequel

Tear Down These Walls is a logical sequel to my previous works. Why was this book written? The conclusion simply stated:

Without a balanced and coherent effort to break down the barriers that hinder access to faith-based behavior, a moral lifestyle and worship cannot be viable in the future. This work is an attempt to prompt faith-based leaders to make reasoned and consistent efforts to remove sectarian and cultural barriers that limit access to personal faith-based expression. Consistent effort must be made to insure attainable adjustments in action and attitude that increases the viability of personal faith and moral lifestyle in a multicultural society. Constant and earnest effort must also be made to weaken the divisions in major monotheistic religions and produce a grassroots response that first creates moral citizens and then enables believers to become a mystical citizen of heaven.

CHAPTER TWO

OVERCOME
HARMFUL CULTURAL PRACTICES

Flying out of Rio de Janeiro, my seatmate was a young Arab graduate student. Not often does an American professor get to talk for an extended period with an intellectual from Syria. A cross-cultural conversation is always a learning experience. A few minutes into the flight, engaging the young man, I asked quietly. "What are your life goals?"

"I have but one goal. My life would be completely fulfilled if I could kill just ten Israelis!" was his abrupt reply. He continued, "I would be willing to give my life in the process of completing this one goal."

How many young Christians would be willing to give their lives in an advancement of a sacred agenda? A single person did not come to mind that would be willing to die for their convictions. That was a tragic conclusion. Nothing remained to talk about. We both read most of the trip. If the door is not open or is closed abruptly, one cannot walk where angels fear to tread.

Translation off – Message Clear

On a trip to Lima, Peru with a missionary group, I was late arriving at the hotel the day of departure. Vessie Hargrave was in charge and told the hotel Doorman, "When Mr. Green comes, tell him we could not wait. He should saddle up his donkey and hurry to the airport." Given the message in Spanish, the Doorman clearly understood, but his English translation was a little off. Arriving ten minutes after the group left, the Doorman rushed up to me with a note. He had made a free translation from Spanish to English: "Mr. Hargrave say, you put ass in saddle and go airport quick." The translation was a little off, but the meaning was clear. Grabbing a cab to make the flight, I shared the note with the group. Everyone had a good laugh. Cross-cultural communication is not easy even on a vacation, but what about dealing with a multicultural community on a serious matter. Multicultural communication becomes a sober challenge to faith-based outreach efforts.

A Shrine to Saint Hollis

Traveling in Peru gathering stories for a magazine, I arrived in Lima the week the Pope removed several saints from the official Vatican list. I searched the streets of Lima seeking someone who could speak English better than I could speak Spanish. Finally, I found a young man about 25 and asked him about the Pope's decision to take certain saints off the list. He said it did not matter, that the people could still pray to those saints, but the church just would not teach the next generation to recognize those removed from the list. I asked, "Why would you want to continue to pray to a saint the Pope says was really not worthy?" The young man responded in effect that the idea of saints was to encourage people to pray; the power was not in the saint, but in the person praying. That was good reasoning, so I pushed the conversation, "What is a saint, and why does the Church select them?" He proceeded to explain that a saint was someone who lived so good and holy that they bypassed Purgatory and went straight to Heaven when they died.

Saint Who?

According to this definition and a theology that did not accept the concept of purgatory, I was a Saint. I stuck out my hand and said, "I am Saint Hollis!" He appeared frightened, but did not say a word. He just turned and walked away rapidly. After a few steps, he turned for another look at me, a few more steps, and turned again. Perhaps he thought I was one of the removed saints who had appeared to him. I observed as he continued toward the Church just down the block where I assumed he would pray or tell his Priest about meeting Saint Hollis.

Saint or Sage

My travels have not taken me back to Lima since that date, but if I were to travel to Lima, I would look on that corner to see if a shrine to Saint Hollis were there. Whether they built a shrine to me or not, sometimes I feel kind of "saintly." My sons say I feel saintly because I am getting old, losing my hair, and my beard has turned white. If not presently known as a "saint," perhaps I have become a "sage." A sage is someone knowledgeable, wise, and experienced, especially a man of advanced years revered for his wisdom and good judgment. Could one be both: a saint for religious faith and a sage for academic adventures? Either way I am satisfied. One young man will remember me, perhaps he built a shrine to "Saint Hollis" in Lima.

A Positive Implies a Negative

In philosophy, a positive implies a negative. Since the positive aspects of culture may be preserved, the converse is true "the harmful practices within a culture may be overcome." Removing that obstacle is a big order. Culture is not static, but is constantly growing, building more walls and accumulating more control over the personal behavior of individuals. Wisdom and experience may enable individuals to make good choices that accentuates the positive and eliminates the negative in their personal lives, but this is rare. External contact with people outside the normal environment, affects cultures. Most cultures do not adequately equip individuals to benefit from interaction with others. It appears that individuals in restrictive cultures do not have a clue that they could break through the negative aspects of their culture and live a different personal life. Positive social change may occur only when individuals understand they can change harmful practices without giving up their basic cultural identity.

Cultural Obstructions

Weakening cultural obstructions may establish the required integrity to influence the public. The elimination of culture and tradition may never be complete, bits and pieces will remain and continue to influence faith-based behavior. The effort is to sanctify these leftovers by removing the sinful elements. This permits a broader and common culture to emerge. Early on the Jerusalem Council made an effort to condense the harmful parts of culture and provide opportunity for Gentile converts to reduce the obstructions and reinforce the moral aspects of their Gentile culture. (Acts 15:28-29)

Emergent Faith-based Culture

Although it appears that faith-based groups of the first century were homogeneous, this was not by design. This happened because of the nature of communities, common customs and the limitation of communication and travels. Although this produced a particular cultural brand of faith, a larger, more comprehensive, even an all-consuming faith-based culture was emerging. The experience transformed their character, made alterations in behavior, and changed their view of others. For example, the Council in Jerusalem sent a letter to Gentile converts declaring:

> For it seemed good to the Holy Spirit and to us, not to impose any extra burden on you, apart from the nec-essary ones; that you abstain from food sacrificed to idols, from tasting blood, from things strangled, and

from sexual immorality; if you guard against these things, you will be doing right. Be strong! (Acts 15:28-29 EDNT)

Homogeneous Groups

The kinship groups and limited travel made the homogeneous groups possible. This suggested sameness or cultural similarity within a congregation as a kind of broad-based homogeneity that does not exist in the multicultural communities today. Dealing with diversity or difference is a basic difficulty for faith-based behavior. A religious organization that attempts to reach coast to coast and border to border cannot achieve sameness. Rather than distinguish the various subcultures and work within an indigenous culture, most faith-based groups seem to strive for universal sameness as an identity. Any sameness should relate to the common ground in sacred writings rather than the specific differences of sectarian groups or local cultures.

Leave Behind Harmful Tradition

Learning to leave behind harmful aspects of religious tradition was an important aspect of early Christianity. Scripture is filled with fishers who forsook their nets to become disciples of a spiritual leader. On one occasion, Jesus called a crowd together and said, *"If anyone wants to follow Me, let him deny himself, and take up his own cross, and come with Me. For whoever wants to save his life will lose it; but whoever loses his life for Me and the gospel, the same will save it.* (Mark 8:34-35 EDNT) Later Saul of Tarsus, a strict Pharisee, gave up much of his religious tradition learned at the feet of Gamaliel (Acts 22:3 EDNT) when he fell from his horse, lost his sight, and left his role as "chief of sinners" behind to become a leader in the very movement he persecuted. This man was trusted to write one-fourth of the New Testament and his words became guiding principles for believers for over two centuries. He encouraged believers to leave behind those aspects of tradition and culture that hindered their growth and development as a witness for the message of grace.

Ethnic Heritage and Cultural Identity

In the first century, believers retained their ethnic heritage and cultural identity as a believer and faithful follower of Jesus; in fact, converts were never required to cross cultural or linguistic barriers to hear the good news of redemption or to sacrifice their heritage or identity. The presentation of the sacred message in the native language in homes and communities within the limitations of culture and tradition reached receptive hearts. Perhaps God never intended to force cultural identity change on individuals: no wonder such attempts creates hostilities and all efforts in this direction constructs barriers to personal faith.

Early believers did not give up their professional or cultural identity to follow Jesus. They operated fishing boats, collected taxes, and retained their identity as Galileans. Luke was a Gentile physician. Paul was a Roman Citizen from Tarsus, trained in the strictness of the Jewish tradition. Barnabas was from Cyprus. Lydia was a proselyte to Judaism working in the business of selling purple. Simon, who carried the cross of Jesus, was a visiting African from Cyrene, and his two sons, Rufus and Alexander, became leaders in the early faith-based movement. A Jew did not give up the Hebrew heritage with a decision to accept the Messiah. A Gentile was not required to become a Jew to embrace a lifestyle of faith and follow others on the Right Path.

Resisting Encroachment of Tradition

One faith-based battle during the first century was the Apostle Paul's effort to protect the Gentile converts from the strong encroachment of Jewish traditions and practices. Although they remained Jewish or Gentile in culture and many aspects of their ethnicity remained the same, converts became something more than their culture; however, they continued to function within their native culture, even within their professions. Converts became a part of a larger cultural environment. It was a beginning; salvation was to separate one from the harmful aspects of their culture and lifestyle not from kindred and natural relationships.

A New and Growing Culture

New believers were a part of a new and growing Messiah-like culture. The objective was to superimpose a larger cultural framework on a community of believers, within which all individuals could function with minimum changes to their basic lifestyle. A faith-based relationship was to separate converts from transgressions fatal to spiritual progress; in other words, from sinful ways, not from their family and friends.

Personal Transformation

As individual believers accepted the basic proposition of faith and morality, there was a personal transformation into a "new creation." In fact, the experience enhanced their established lifestyle. For example, the soldiers who converted to the new Way remained in the military, but moral principles guided them not to abusing their authority. New believers were to abide in their present calling to influence their associates, colleagues and friends. The conversion of Zaccheus, a Jericho tax collector, brought a change of lifestyle and a moral element to his profession. He made restitution for wrongs and became a donor to the poor. This was a drastic change since the people of Jericho saw Zaccheus as a man who habitually did wrong.

A Divine Encounter

Often a divine encounter became an intervention that brought the good news to both individuals and groups. On one occasion, first century Jews from many nations gathered in Jerusalem for a Religious Feast. The time had come for the rapid expansion of the new Way; consequently, God intervened. There was no time for extensive language training or cross-cultural preparation for missionary evangelism. The Holy Spirit enabled believers to articulate an unnaturally acquired language and witness of the *wonderful works of God.* In Jerusalem individuals from various nations and languages, received the witness of God's grace in their native language. (Acts 2:4-12 EDNT) The multicultural society existing then seems similar to the multifaceted culture present in many communities today. Instead of waiting for a divine encounter that enables faith to work, some groups attempt to manipulate the people and the culture to achieve their goals; consequently, the forced effort ends in relative failure and more walls are constructed. Common sense teaches that when a process is broken, the effort to fix the problem should be forth coming.

Manipulation vs. Motivation

Attempting to get others to do what you want them to do is manipulation, while motivation is "motive" plus "action" and requires an understanding of the motives of others in order to provide an action or a way to achieve personal goals. Most people desire to be free from past sins and have a hopeful future. Forgiveness is a big issue in religion. The quality of family life and the nature of life after death is a concern for most adults. Mercy, amnesty, and pardon are the wishes of individuals burdened with habitual wrong behavior. Any hope of change in a community must offer a way to reach these personal goals. A fresh understanding of how to walk the Right Path to redemption is a priority in all faith-based advancement.

Identified by Culture and Location

Historically the identification of faith-based congregations were known through the culture of a particular location. This was an essential element in pristine movements and worked well in a world with restricted mobility and limited association with outsiders. Each local gathering of believers was a part of some larger more comprehensive group; such as, the gathered church in Jerusalem, Antioch, Corinth, Ephesus, Rome, or the churches of Asia. Each house of worship was recognized and presented in sacred writings as people of a particular village, town, or region of a country. Location, not dogma, was the principle point of identification. Collectively, the houses of worship in a particular area constituted the gathered church for that region and were associated with believers in other places. Sadly, this natural connection created the constructs for sectarian separation based on difference. Permitting similarities to unite eventually identified differences that caused division. Ignoring the social construct that commonalities unite, but differences divide has become a limiting factor in faith-based unity.

A Cultural Framework

A system of belief created in a cultural framework dominates most of the sectarian divisions in religion. The perpetuators of sectarian divisions appear to be obstinately devoted to tradition, personal opinions and prejudices. This enables discrimination and hatred arising from attaching value to perceived differences between people. This creates a brand name identity for places of worship established on a culturally based body of teachings. This was true even of the early followers of Jesus, the Galilean. It appears most of his early followers were from Galilee. All the original twelve disciples were Galileans. Most of the 120 in the Upper Room celebration were Galileans and the perception on the Day of Pentecost was clear "are not all these who speak Galileans."

Modern faith-based groups are more interested in their system of belief and form of government than any connection with the local community. Organized religion fails to join the interest or purpose of the people of a particular environment and have no way of knowing the degree to which their programs receive approval except by negative participation. Yet, when the people do not participate, they continue the programs as if each manmade program was God ordered and ordained and must continue. Always some higher, more pressing agenda imposes both method and message on the people rather than meeting the needs of the community. Local congregations seem to have no partnership, no walking together or joining forces to meet the needs or aspirations of the people. Each faith-based group requires the people to adapt to their particular agenda whether it meets their needs or not. This builds a psychological wall between faith-based groups and potential participants.

Common Tenets vs. Lowest Common Denominator

This is not to suggest that the world needs a lowest common denominator religion. Rather, it is to point to the power of personal faith and the need to emphasize common tenets that bring people together. Social and cultural differences will always exist in religious groups, but there is common ground. A gathered congregation is a social institution, and faith-based worship should be a force to unite rather than divide. The human factor will always complicate the universal values of a spiritual outreach. Individuals will not move toward faith when the message or the method attempts to extract them from their local culture. Scripture predicted in Isaiah that the *"highway of holiness would be so plain that no traveler would err."* Believers must find their comfort zone and behave their faith in the social context of their own environment and walking with believers on the Right Path and functioning without sectarian walls.

Rise Above Petty Differences

Multicultural limitations normally do not hinder at times of national crisis or celebration. During wars and other times of crisis individuals people from different cultures, occupations, professions, or social class join together to restore peace and tranquility to the lives of their countrymen. In civilized nations, the political parties lay aside their differences after elections briefly to affect a peaceful transfer of power. Individuals rise above petty differences to the commonalties of citizenship. It would assist the message of grace if faith-based groups would present themselves as a community of believers in One God and accentuate the sharing of common moral values. Without such observed common ground, there can be no true witness of grace to a community. At times diversity may have value, but in sharing a faith-based message there must be observable unity. If groups cannot overcome petty differences, why should others become involved?

Grow Beyond Sectarian Dogma

To make religion viable, each believer must grow beyond fixed sectarian dogma and become part of the universal faith-based movement and be ready, willing and able to practice a personal faith in their own home base. Opposition to religion is well organized and united in an effort to eliminate faith-based behavior from society. Brand name religion that segregates believers into cubicles based on dogma will never produce a sufficient number of viable witnesses to fulfill the commission to make disciples. Minimize differences and emphasize the common ground in order to produce cooperation and unity among people of faith. Differences divide; commonalities unite. To make a faith-based community viable, cultural differences must not distract from the One God message. True faith will demonstrate that the Right Path passes by every home and through ever village and town and is not limited by heritage, race, culture, tradition, or social standing.

A Pathway Forward

Most faith-based groups seem more interested in advancing culturally based teaching that supports a particular brand of religion, than connecting with the human needs of a local community. When a belief system does not join the interest of a particular locale, it sows the seeds of failure. When a brand of faith does not meet the adverbs of necessity demonstrated by the community, faith-based groups have little spiritual viability or force for positive social change.

One of my graduate students, a college teacher from Taiwan, was having difficulty choosing a dissertation topic. Inquiry about the problems of students in The Republic of China produced a clear and firm response, "Some students desire to embrace Christianity but do not want to give up their Chinese heritage." Moving the discussion forward, she made a list of theological terms and then wrote them pictorially. The first one was "redemption." She began by explaining what the old pictographs meant. "Writing it the ancient way, redemption is a man under a lamb." Her conclusion was that deeply rooted in Chinese culture was the concept of redemption and ransom related to a lamb. This presented a way forward and an approach to her college students. They could accept ransom and redemption by a Lamb from God embedded in the pre-Christian culture of the Chinese people. They could retain their Chinese identity without embracing a new culture. It was clear that accepting redemption based on their historic roots was the Right Path forward and a way to reduce cultural distractions.

CHAPTER THREE

REDUCE CULTURAL DISTRACTIONS

Speaking in a Maryland Community Church on the subject of "Living a Separated Life" was a learning experience. Each time the message reached the point that God expected believers to live a clean, pure, separated life an elderly man in the back would stand and say, "Call him John, Brother." After a few incidents of this, my confusion grew trying to figure out what the man meant. Not being familiar with dialogical preaching, finally it dawned on me that this was a community gathering and the congregation included several groups. Perhaps this man was an old Methodist who knew about the Doctrine of Sanctification. The next time the phrase, "God expects believers to live a clean pure and separated life" it was added that the old Methodist called this behavior living the sanctified life. At this, the old man jumped to his feet and said, "If his name is John, call him John!" He was coaching me to use old theological terms, such as "sanctification," instead of describing the behavior of a sanctified life. It all came out OK. The man was able to get the term "sanctification" into the sermon and the message described the lifestyle of living a clean, pure and separated life. It was a cultural distraction and brought the reality that old words often do not inform current behavior.

Choice of Words

In the public square and in the arena of faith there is an effort to be politically correct in the choice of words. Words are important, but the true meaning of words is in people. The dictionary provides academics with working definitions and the study of languages enhances the meanings, but words mean different things to different people. The real meaning of words is in people and the meaning is colored by culture and life experience. Consequently, the choice of words is important.

Words can Distract

America and England are two countries separated by a common language. This creates apprehension for travelers. One year, an Oxford academic, Geoffrey Thomas, Ph.D., spoke at the Oxford Graduate School Degree Day in Tennessee. He shared an example of the problem with language. It seems that when an Englishman uses "momentarily" the word means "for a moment," but when an American uses the same word it means "in a moment." Dr. Thomas asked, "Can you imagine how I felt when the American pilot said we will be taking off momentarily? I thought we will go up and immediately back down!" Following this event, a dictionary of terms was created for students traveling to England. For example:

- A library card is a ticket.
- An elevator is a lift.
- A truck is a lorry.
- A single home is a detached house.
- A duplex is a semi-detached house.
- An apartment is a flat.
- A car's trunk is a boot.
- A car's hood is a bonnet.
- A windshield is a windscreen.
- A car's fuel is petrol.
- A cookie is a biscuit.
- A paper plate is a cardboard plate.

- A drugstore is a Chemist.
- A 4-lane is a dual carriageway.
- A highway is a motorway.
- A letter is posted.
- A car is hired, not rented.
- A car driven on the left is on the correct side.
- A person's weight is measured in stones.
- And the list goes on...

Different Kind of Cultural Distraction

Traveling in the Asia/Pacific area, I experienced a different kind of cultural distraction. Arriving three days early in Hong Kong for a much needed rest, a voice in the airport shocked me, "Brother Green is that you?" It was a missionary from the Philippines. His second question was, "Where are you staying? I will change hotels so we can talk." Living in another culture as a missionary, he was longing for a comfortable and informal conversation between friends. He came to my room and talked until after midnight. It is good to talk with people from back home who share common culture and faith.

The next day the decision to go shopping was a learning experience. The closed shops on a Chinese Religious Holiday changed my plans. My promise to buy a British Racing Cap and a sleeveless cashmere sweater vest for a friend was in jeopardy. Closed shops did not douse my desire to shop, my decision was to window shop to pass the time "alone." Looking in the window of a shop that carried the desired items and feeling somewhat discouraged since my departure from Hong Kong would occur before the shops opened, a well-dressed man outside the shop asked, "Do you wish to purchase something?" "Yes, but the shop is closed," was the response.

The man claimed to be the shop owner and would take my order and ship it to my home. He honored the holiday, but was concerned about his personal business. Sharing the items including the sizes, he asked for my mailing address and said it would cost $37.18. Without thinking, an exchange of money for the order completed the transaction. Returning to the hotel wondering how stupid can one be giving money to a stranger on the street, the Concierge at the hotel became aware of my action. He asked for my address and the amount paid to the merchant and wrote a personal guarantee, "If you do not receive the merchandise within 21 days, I will personally send you the $37.18. Hong Kong merchants are the most honest businessmen in the world. This is a positive aspect of their culture upon which they built their business."

The religious holiday that closed the shops was a distraction, but in less than 3-weeks a package came from Hong Kong with the merchandise and a small envelop. The package contained a note and 17 cents. It seems the merchant had overestimated the postage. I could hardly believe such integrity exhibited by a stranger on the street. This event changed my attitude toward people of other faiths and initiated the process of questioning the integrity of the message sent by faith-based behavior in the marketplace.

Positive Social and Spiritual Change

Could my friends express such integrity in the marketplace and elicit such trust by a stranger as did this Chinese merchant? Can we keep faith-based people from cheating on their taxes? Can we keep a butcher from weighting his thumb? Can we keep the Landlord from overcharging the poor? Can we stop the cheating spouse? Can we eliminate abortion? Can faith-based groups remove the barriers of insincerity, hypocrisy, and dishonesty? Can different religions learn from each other? How can atheists and polytheistic people practice a morality in certain areas of life that faith-based people find difficult if not impossible? Does conversion and regeneration still transform the moral aspects of human behavior? If the above questions have affirmative answers, why not more aggressive action from faith-based groups to bring about positive social and spiritual change in the community.

Elements of a Common Culture

After the time of Jesus, His Way brought people together into a common lifestyle from a wide diversity of races, cultures and other religious backgrounds. Early believers developed the elements of a common culture that served as an umbrella simultaneously for many subcultures. When converts began to walk the new path, some of their lifestyle and practices changed, but not all. Converts remained and functioned within their native culture, but identified with the larger faith-based community. When the respect for native culture of each convert was not forthcoming, spiritual leaders intervened. An example is Paul's contention with Peter over an attempt to impose Jewish ways on Gentile converts. (Galatians 2:11-14)

Accentuate Common Ground

Little effort to understand various cultures and accentuate the common ground exists among people of faith. This failure enhances the effect of differences rather than the common ground. The emphasis on difference divides the message into so many parts that the public cannot construct the whole. Could this explain the lack of scriptural literacy? Much of scriptural meaning is lost in the assorted interpretations. Only a common message can advance human understanding of faith, yet faith-based groups constantly emphasize their differences. This dissimilarity is a tragic flaw that divides the faith-based community and presents a misleading message. Sadly, this continues as if the process of building walls and keeping secrets were an asset. This is a drawback to the public understanding of faith-based behavior and a liability to individual and group cooperation in areas where there should be common ground. A cultural framework for faith-based groups has created a brand name concept for faith and worship that was based on distinctive teachings of the past.

Public Identity Crisis

The attempt to distinguish one faith-based group from another based on distinctive teachings does not adequately present the monotheistic faith to the public. In fact, it breaks down the quality of the whole group by an emphasis on a multifaceted message. Emphasis on differences to distinguish one group from another is to distort the general impression of the faith-based movement. The public has a right to assume that a faith-based group would be "Messiah-like" and share the same or similar teachings with other groups that claim to be a part of the same whole. To be whole, all parts must be included. When significant differences in the various groups are evident, the public begins to question the validity of the whole.   This creates a public identity crisis for the faith-based lifestyle. Could this be a strategy of the enemy of faith? Could this be the reason for warring and strife in the realm of religion?

Strategy of the Enemy

Confusion exists among religious groups as to the differences between being distinct and being distinctive. Part of the problem is a lack of understanding of the idea of being distinct. To be distinct is to be dissimilar and clearly seen. On the other hand, to be distinctive is to be one not commonly found elsewhere and suggests exclusivity. When a faith-based group believes themselves to be distinctive, they normally possess the concept of exclusivity. In this way, they separate themselves from other faith-based groups, and become incompatible with other believers and are unable to exist together, at the same time, or in the same place. This brings disharmony and even antagonistic feelings among people who claim to worship the same Deity. It appears that such divisiveness is an evil strategy to divide and conquer. Small differences should not produce exclusivity or disharmony. It is clear that cultural expressions can differ when dealing with the same truth. Mature human beings should understand this, especially if they claim to be committed to spiritual matters.

Differences Exist

The concept of identity is one of being identical or having sameness; however, differences exist within individuals or groups that are part of the same whole. Even identical twins that develop from a single egg and are the same gender have differences. Scholars note identical twins for sameness not for almost indistinguishable difference. The appearance is so similar that only close relatives can recognize the differences. It should be this way with the faith-based community. Those who are a part of the inner circle may see the differences and understand the causes for a different perspective or explanation, but the public should never have to sort through a jumbled message. Even when faith wears cultural clothes, a unified message of basic faith and common grace is necessary for public understanding.

Population of Heaven

The differences are usually not consequential enough to change the population of heaven. Individual views of particular aspects of scripture may exist, but a central theme and message is present. Distortion of this common message by sectarian analysis will confuse the public. If the different perspective of a particular part of scripture is not significant enough to change the population of heaven, it should not confuse the message of grace or produce disharmony within the band of believers.

Sameness Determines Identity

A family is a group that is similar and connected. This sameness causes a blending of mind and heart. Certainly, a family has differences, but the members of the primary group associate freely with each other and is characterized by similarities. One may speak of a family circle when describing close relatives or a family tree when describing how individuals are connected. They have a sameness that determines the family identity. Differences in the background are acceptable, as new members are welcomed into the larger family circle. Whether it is the family photo album or a genealogical chart, sameness makes the kinship association. Has faith-based groups lost the concept of family? Is there no sameness? Must each group present a distinctive message to the world and project a divided movement? The people of earth deserve a simple and clear message of grace from the Family of God.

The Third Strand

The fabric of families is made up of divergent strands which come together to make a single unit. It seems that two strands may be twisted together to form yarn for use in creating fabric, but at least three strands are required to braid or plait a strong and useful thread. Two strands alone cannot form a strong union; a third stand is required to provide strength for the unit. In the case of a couple coming together in marriage, this third strand is a sense of family that permeates the commitment and supplies the adhesive for a strong bond. The wise man Solomon said, "Two are better than one and a cord with three strands is not quickly broken." It is the third strand that Solomon considered the strength of the union. The common message of faith and grace must be a vital part of the faith-based movement or the credibility of the whole is in jeopardy. A common message of love, mercy, and forgiveness must form the third strand and provide strength for fellowship.

Vitality in Common Ground

The same is true of religious groups, when one faith-based group attempts to stand alone or limit association with a few who are "just the same," the binding strand which brings strength is missing. There is some value in diversity, but there is energy and strength in common ground. Groups that insist on projecting dissimilarity will remain weak without a sense of commitment to commonalties that could inform their participation in the larger community of faith. Sectarian groups that isolate themselves from the whole by emphasizing the distinctive nature of a particular teaching rather than a common identity with the community of faith will suffer limitations and remain earthen vessels without the spiritual dynamic to bring a faith-based reality to the world. Individual believers must study sacred writings in search of the common message of grace.

Differences Divide and Weaken

There is strength in unity and weakness in division. Holy scripture was clear, "If a house is divided against itself, that house cannot stand." This was in the context of the reality that Satan would never permit division in his work. Perhaps these differences within faith-based groups proceed from an evil scheme to perpetuate division.

No reasonable explanation or course of action exists that eliminate the possibility of true conversion to the pristine faith. Differences with secondary importance are similar to the "little foxes" that Solomon warned about. The little foxes destroyed the fruit by eating the blossoms and the tender grapes. It is obvious that the faith-based cause must be on guard against enemies as sly and cunning as any fox that will destroy the fruit bearing ability of faith-based groups. Early disciples were told:

1. I am the true and genuine vine, and My Father is the vine-dresser. 2. He destroys every unfruitful branch in Me: and every branch that bears fruit, He cleans so it may bring forth more fruit. 3. Now you have been cleansed through the word which I spoke to you. 4. Abide in Me, and I in you. As the branch cannot bear fruit from itself, except it abide in the vine; no more can you bear fruit, except you abide in Me. 5. I am the vine, you are the branches: He who abides in Me, and I in him, the same brings forth much fruit: for apart from Me you can do nothing. 6. If a man does not abide in Me, he is cast out of the vineyard as the unfruitful branch and is dried up; and they gather and burn them. 7. If you abide in Me, and My words abide in you, you ask what you will, and it will come to pass for you. 8. My Father was glorified in this, that you bear much fruit; and you shall become My disciples. (John 15:1-8 EDNT)

Searching the Scriptures

In addition to personal devotional reading and study, each believer needs to listen carefully to the sharing and teaching ministry of a local assembly. Listening may not mean taking notes; in fact, most people can learn more by disciplined listening and doing follow-up study based on the shared passage of scripture. The believers in Berea were good listeners and good students of the Word *They received the word with all readiness of mind, and searched the scriptures daily* (Acts 17:11). Private study alone is not sufficient for spiritual growth. Each believer needs the guidance of the Holy Spirit and the fellowship of other believers. At times, this guidance comes through a local spiritual leader; at other times it comes through prayer and meditation as one shares their personal study of the Word with family and friends.

Product of Culture

Sadly the differences that divide the faith-based community are the product of human culture and have produced stumbling blocks to accepting the message of grace. Constant and earnest effort is required to search out these barriers to the witness of faith. Scripture is clear that God overlooked the past lack of understanding and opened a new door to faith.

22. And standing in the center of the Areopagus, Paul said, Men of Athens, I perceive that in all things you are fearful of deities. 23. For as I passed through your city and saw the objects of your worship, I found an altar inscribed, TO AN UNKNOWN GOD. The One you unknowingly worship, I announce to you. 24. The God who ordered the universe and all the things in it, the One being Lord of heaven and earth does not dwell in hand made shrines; 25. neither is He served by human hands, as though He needed something from man, seeing He gives to all life, breath, and all things; 26. and has made of one blood all nations of men who dwell on the earth, determined the history of nations and their territory; 27. so they should search for God and hopefully find Him although He is not far from all of us. 28. For in Him we live and move, and have our being; as certain also of your own poets have said, For we are also His offspring. 29. Since we are the offspring of God, we ought not to think that the Deity has any similarity to anything made of gold, silver, or stone that is sculptured by the art and imagination of man. 30. Then God overlooked this past lack of knowledge, but now commands all men everywhere to repent: 31. because he has set aside a day in which he will judge the world with justice by the Man He has chosen and has provided assurance to mankind by standing Him up from among the dead. (Acts 17: 22-31 EDNT)

CHAPTER FOUR

REMOVE BEHAVIORAL STUMBLING BLOCKS

Weddings are trying times because there are so many things to do with so many telling others how to do them. At a wedding rehearsal with Carolyn and Jerry Bare, going over the parts that the bride and groom were to repeat, I read, "Do you take this woman whose hand you hold to be your lawful wedded wife, for better or worse; for richer or poorer; in sickness and in health..." As the groom selected better, richer, health...the rehearsal was stopped and the groom reminded that the marriage ceremony was not multiple choice. It was all or nothing. You cannot have the milk unless you buy the whole cow. The groom responded, "You can't fault a man for trying." Perhaps this is human nature based on culture and tradition. However, the obligations of life are to be taken freely without any mental reservation or purpose of evasion.

Old Predispositions

This event makes one aware that some individuals in love with their previous life and limited obligations may permit one to hold on to old predispositions that become stumbling blocks to the peace and tranquility of home and hearth. Could this be the real problem in modern family life? Could old attitudes influence members in faith-based groups? If so, we should encourage everyone to accept and fulfill all obligations and responsibility to society and in particular to personal and family life. This may also be instructive in weak conversions when individuals accept membership with mental reservation or personal evasion and do not fully embrace the relational aspects of a faith-based lifestyle.

Dysfunctional Behavior

Many marriages fail because of dysfunctional behavior, the same is true of faith-based groups that are weakened by both the failure to follow normal procedures, as well as improper action or the immoral behavior of members. Tragically, there is similarity between the union of two humans in marriage and membership in a faith-based group. Since both the clergy and the congregation are composed of human beings, an attachment to a local assembly is also considered to be a social union influenced by tradition, culture, and various human dynamics. Accepting personal responsibility for moral behavior and basic support are similar to accepting the marriage vows and joining a religious congregation. The social union aspects of marriage made complex by traditions and customs vary between groups and are problematical because of human nature. In both cases, there are promises and declarations concerning love, honor, and conformity.

Broken Promises

Unfortunately, when these promises are broken there is mental severance, criticism, condemnation, and ultimately dissolution of the relationship. The process of undoing or breaking this bond comes in many forms of dysfunctional behavior; such as, adding another to adulterate a relationship, personal animosity, abandonment, annulment, or a final termination of the relationship. The process is similar to impeachment in government, ecclesiastical censure and excommunication, or legal separation and divorce in marriage. Regardless of the nature of sundering, or the names used to describe the process, the results are the same.

8. These things are faithful sayings that I want you to affirm confidently, that the believers in God might be careful to maintain good deeds. These things are good and profitable to all men. 9. But avoid foolishly searching for family pedigrees, and arguments and ruthlessness about the law; for they serve no useful purpose for anyone. 10. A man that holds to belief that contradicts these things after the second warning avoid his company; 11. you must know that such a man is perverted and under self-condemnation. (Titus 3: 8-11 EDNT)

Scandalous Behavior

A reported comment of Gandhi about Christians is telling, he said, "I like your Christ. I do not like your Christians. They are so unlike your Christ." Behavior that causes others to stumble is scandalous. The Greek word for "offend" actually mean "to cause to stumble, entrap, trip up or entice to sin." The English word for "offend" is to scandalize. To permit personal behavior to weaken the young or offend is disgraceful, immoral, shameful, and shocking. True believers will not forsake the basic teachings of scripture and become involved in scandalous behavior. Early spiritual leaders saw that offending others was a serious matter. Consequently, disciplined behavior is a necessary step in spiritual progress. Notice below the true consequence of causing another to stumble or enticing them to sin. This clearly points to the urgency of removing wrong behavior from the faith-based community either by restoration to the right path or removal from public view.

41. For whoever gives you a cup of water to drink in My name, because you belong to Christ, I assure you, he will not lose his wages. 42. And whoever shall cause to stumble or entice to sin one of these little ones who believes in Me, it is better for him that a large grinder-stone be wrapped around his neck, and be thrown into the sea. (Mark 9:41-42 DNT)

Stumbling Blocks

An obstacle or stumbling block is a predisposition to act that leads another to careless and destructive living. The actions, deeds, and deportment of individuals who claim membership in faith-based group will become a bad example and destructive role model for others. To maintain a viable witness in any community, faith-based leaders must remove behavioral stumbling blocks and restore the individual to a moral lifestyle. Sacred scripture is clear that no one should do anything to cause another to stumble or fall into sin.

> 11. It is in scripture, As surely as I live, every knee will bow before Me, and every tongue shall acknowledge God. 12. So then every one of us shall give account of himself to God. 13. Let us stop passing judgment on one another: but rather determine that no man will do anything to cause his brother to stumble and fall. (Romans 14:13 EDNT)

Unable to Transcend Religiosity

Faith-based leaders must personally embrace the principles that strengthen the confidence of followers. Often the choice is not to follow faith-based principles in personal conduct. In most cases, the essence of the faith is not used as a basis for reasoning or behavior. Faith-based groups have been unable to transcend habitual religiosity or the performance of required tasks and have failed to develop the compelling ideas, which transcend the scheduled program. This leads to parents who fail to go beyond the day-to-day functioning of the family and never bring their children to a conceptual level of faith and spiritual function.

Absent Role Models

Some local worshippers fail to bear witness to the behavior appropriate for those who claim membership in a faith-based group. There is little effort to affirm moral and ethical behavior as a model; in fact, the public conduct and private behavior of some folk suggests that the opposite is acceptable. Positive role models are absent, and little effort made to support those who rise above the standards of an immoral society. The public receives more information on heroes and champions from the secular press than from faith-based leaders. This must change!

Accountability for Behavior

To err is an essential aspect of being human; however, those who profess a faith-based life and violate accepted moral standards of conduct must be accountable. Those guilty of unacceptable conduct weaken the faith-based witness and become a obstacle to potential converts. The veracity of the personal witness must be restored to make faith-based groups viable. Recognized objectionable behaviors that becomes a stumbling block are animosity, arrogance, egotism, idleness, immorality, resentment, and self-indulgence.

Animosity – When hostility, hatred and bitterness are present, the faith-based witness suffers.

Arrogance – When conceit, superiority and pride are obvious, moral influence is diminished.

Egotism – When insensitivity and boastfulness are demonstrated, the moral cause of faith is weakened.

Idleness – When laziness and inactivity are evident, any faith-based mission will fail.

Immorality – When depravity and wickedness are flaunted, moral corruption will flourish.

Resentment – When conflict and competition are displayed, there is little hope for spiritual progress.

Self-indulgence – When extravagance and unrestrained gratification are apparent, all effort for positive social change is lost.

In addition to the list above, sacred scripture details the behavior that will become a stumbling block to others:

19. Now the behavior that belongs to the flesh is obvious, they are: (sensual sins) unfaithfulness in marriage, unrestrained living, unbridled acts of indecency; 20. (religious sins) the worship of idols, the use of drugs and magical powers, (temperamental sins) hostility, strife, jealousy, violent flare ups of temper, self-seeking ambitions, adherence to contradictory teaching, 21.(personal sins) desires to appropriate what others have, drunkenness and carousing, and similar things: I warned you before that people who do such things will have no part in the kingdom of God. (Galatians 5:19-21 EDNT)

Assist in Removing Stumbling Blocks

Although private devotional reading and study are important, they are no substitute for the teaching ministry of the Holy Spirit (John 16:13-15), nor does private devotional study replace believers assembling together for worship (Hebrews 10:23-25) or for witnessing and sharing (Acts 1:8). Worship and knowledge of the Word can assist in removing behavioral stumbling blocks. When believers are fully instructed and convinced of the foundational truths of sacred scripture their attitude and behavior would not be a stumbling block to others. When a weak one stumbles, it is required of the strong to assist with recovery back to a stable spiritual walk. Remember, a stumble is an unsteady step with a surprise slip normally followed by a few quick steps to keep from falling. This is where mature believers enter the picture, following the stumble, believers help with the few quick steps to get the weak one back on track. In sacred writings, the Letter to the Galatians clearly points out the need for direct action and an effort to spiritual restore those with objectionable and offensive conduct:

*1. Brethren, if a man should make **an unintended error due to weakness, you who are regenerated, repair and adjust him with a teachable spirit;** continue considering yourself, lest you also be tempted to make a false step. 2. Practice in sharing the heavy burdens of others, and you will fulfill the principle of Christ. 3. If a man supposes himself to be something when he is really nothing, he deceives himself. 4. Let every man test himself for innocence, and then he shall rejoice in himself and not in another. 5. For every man must carry his own personal load. 6. Let him who receives instructions in the word share in support of the teacher's living. 7. Be not deceived; no man can avoid God: for whatever a man may sow this also he will reap; 8. for he who plants proceeds in the field of the material shall have a spoiled harvest; but he who plants proceeds in the field of the spiritual life shall harvest life everlasting. 9. **And let us not become weary in doing what is right: for if we do not weaken our resolve, in due season we will collect the good harvest. 10. As we have opportunity, let us practice generosity to all, especially to those who are of the congregation of faith.** (Galatians 6:1-10 EDNT)*

Does it Matter?

Does it matter whether one calls water baptism a sacrament or an ordinance? Why does confusion exist in relation to baptism? Within the faith-based community, the observance of baptism is for different reasons and performed by different methods. For some it is an act of purification, for others it is one of public separation of the old lifestyle, still others see water baptism as an act of initiation into Faith or identification with the Godhead. Notwithstanding the true purpose of baptism, the mode is of more concern to some than the actual purpose of act or public obedience to a scriptural command. Controversy actually exists over whether the baptismal water may be still or must be running. Will the mode of baptism change the population of heaven? Are these differences sufficient cause to divide the Congregaion of Believers? Is the mode or the act of obedience on the part of individuals the essential matter? Are these differences and divisions worth the muddled message they send to the public? Can the faith-based message be viable when such variation in basic understanding exists among the faithful? From the viewpoint of eternity, does the method of immersion versus sprinkling make a significant difference?

Argument over Baptism

There is a story of two rural ministers discussing the mode of baptism: it seems the Baptist insisted on total immersion and the Methodist thought the act of sprinkling was sufficient. They did agree: it was not the amount of water, but what the water covered that made the difference. Water up to the knees, waist, or even to the neck was not sufficient for the Baptist, if the water did not cover the forehead or top of the head it was not a valid baptism. The argument was simple: the water must cover the head. The Methodist countered, "You mean if the water covers everything on a person but the forehead it is not a sufficient baptism?" The Baptist agreed. The Methodist contended since covering the forehead was what ultimately counted, he used the method of sprinkling to be sure to get the forehead wet. This is a ridiculous story and has little to do with the purpose of baptism or the population of heaven, but it points out the nature of insignificant differences.

A Lack of Inclusiveness

The uncertain sound of the gospel trumpet does not rally the troops within the church or cause much concern outside the walls. Worship has degenerated to entertainment to attract attendance, but religious services cannot compete with television, movies, or the offerings of the Internet. Another factor is that the constructs of faith and a moral lifestyle have been placed in the ambiguity of the English language that has an either/or complex and leaves wiggle room in matters of faith and practice. This leads to a lack of inclusiveness and breeds the construction of a polytheistic lifestyle with dependence on many god-like forces. Any person, object, or imagination comes before God becomes an idol god and demands adoration and affection. Regardless of one's claim to worship One God, attachment to such god-like entities as wealth and fame moves a person into the polytheistic realm.

CHAPTER FIVE

DEMOLISH POLYTHEISTIC TRADITIONS

Early monotheistic religions developed in a polytheistic world, but first thrived in a common culture before diversifying. Judaism began with the family of Abraham within the Hebrew language and culture; Christianity first grew among the Galileans in Palestine, and used Greek and Aramaic as a language; Islam began in the Arabian Peninsula and in the Arabic language, *Islam* means "submission" to God and a person who submits and follows Islam is called a *Muslim*. Each monotheistic faith developed within a common culture that served as an umbrella simultaneous for other sub-cultures as different traditions became part of their faith. When individuals accepted a religion, some of their lifestyle and practices changed but not all. The converts remained and functioned within their native culture, but identified with the larger cultural community. This gradually changed both the religion and the people involved.

Shaped by Culture and Tradition

As the religions grew they brought people together into a common life from a diversity of races, cultures and other traditions. Early places of worship were houses and involved whole families. Monotheistic religions, as organized entities, express themselves in local gatherings and owe much in their history to many people other than the professional elite. Many made significant contributions to the cause: scholars, writers, artists, architects, soldiers, and historians. There were both saints and scientists, philosophers with ideas and men of action. The formation of faith-based leadership came by both the culture and by an understanding of the faith.

Conversion and a Call

Leadership was defined in faith-based groups while the faith movements were still persecuted minorities, long before local congregations entered partnership with civil and organized society. Clerics and lay leaders were not born to the role. Each future leader was born an amateur, some outside the influence of the faith itself. This required both a conversion and a call to open the door to spiritual leadership. Despite the various names used by different groups: clergy, priest, presbyter, pastor, minister, imam or rabbi, all the religious leadership performs the same basic functions of teaching and guidance in the specialized dogma of the group. Inside their particular congregation, they possessed real authority. Some are a representative or agent of God, while others are mere messengers and devout adherents. A democratic process at times may limit their authority, but it is there. Nevertheless, they maintain the authority to perform the rites of their exclusive order or group and to exercise leadership in certain spheres within the group and sometimes in a larger faith community.

Devotion to Many Gods

Individuals who do not truly believe in the **one and only God, Creator and Sustainer of the Universe** usually end up creating their own idols and individual gods. People without a true faith and loyalty to One God, often worship many gods or idols, some they even fashioned by hand. Some people; such as, the Romans, transformed their head of government into a "god" and offered worship and praise to this man as a deity. During the historic periods of the Greek and Roman cultures, which were not monotheistic, the culture developed many idols and gods and worshipped the creature more than the Creator. People, who have no real personal commitment to the cardinal tenets of the faith, fostered by an Almighty God, often embrace constructs that are polytheistic and conjure up their own personal and false gods together with a pseudo-theology for self-defense.

24. The God who ordered the universe and all the things in it, the One being Lord of heaven and earth does not dwell in hand made shrines; 25. neither is He served by human hands, as though He needed something from man, seeing He gives to all life, breath, and all things; 26. and has made of one blood all nations of men who dwell on the earth, determined the history of nations and their territory; 27. so they should search for God and hopefully find Him although He is not far from all of us. 28. For in Him we live and move, and have our being; as certain also of your own poets have said, For we are also His offspring. 29. Since we are the offspring of God, we ought not to think that the Deity has any similarity to anything made of gold, silver, or stone that is sculptured by the art and imagination of man. (Acts 17:24-29 EDNT)

Engineered Constructs

In creating a world of false religions and humanistic philosophies, the human race engineered many constructs to explain their view of the world and their understanding of a Higher Power. History has become an age of "isms" and the creation of words using "ism" as a suffix. These are characterized by at least seven (7) social "isms that influence religion:" agnosticism, capitalism, communism, hedonism, humanism, materialism, and narcissism; among other things.

Agnosticism – a philosophical view that expresses uncertainty about the existence of God;

Capitalism – a political philosophy and economic theory that suggests a kind of individualism where people own things not a government;

Communism – a socialist movement to create a classless, moneyless, and stateless social order and structure;

Hedonism – a philosophical position that takes the pursuit of pleasure as the only intrinsic good and that primary human activity leads to self-indulgent, pleasure-seeking, and self-gratification;

Humanism – a progressive philosophy that rejects religious beliefs and centers on humans and their values, capacities, and worth;

Materialism – a theory that physical matter is the fundamental reality and that all being and processes and phenomena can be explained as manifestations or results of matter and often expresses itself in greed, covetousness, and excessive desire for wealth or gain;

Narcissism – an inordinate fascination with self, pride, conceit, arrogance and self-importance;

8. Howbeit then, when you were ignorant of God you were in bondage to gods that were not gods at all. 9. But now after you learned to know God and God knows you, how turn you again to the weak and childish teachings, desiring again to be in a condition of servitude? 10. Observing days, months, times, and years. 11. I am fearful that my labor on your behalf was wasted. 12. Brethren walk in liberty as I do for I was once in bondage as you are: (Galatians 4:8-12 EDNT)

A Philosopher's Definition of God

I became aware of a philosopher's definition of God while traveling alone down Interstate 75, south of Atlanta. The long journey ahead suggested a hitchhiker might be good company. As the young man entered the car, "Good morning, my name is Hollis Green, I am a Christian." The response was, "Carl Krudof, I am a philosopher." Baiting the young philosopher, "Do you write your philosophy down, or do you just talk? He claimed to write important thoughts down. This interested me. "What have you written lately?" Carl responded, "I have just written a definition of God, but I don't believe there is one."

[A definition of God by a philosopher who doesn't believe in God. This was going to be interesting.]

Reaching into the back seat to retrieve a small-unzipped notebook, Carl began to read: "God is the singular, possessive, abstraction of the adverb."

[He IS a philosopher; my teachers talked that way. Carl was asked to repeat the definition.]

He repeated, "God is the singular, possessive abstraction of the adverb.

[What is an adverb? I have been out of school too long.]

Carl continued, "An adverb is the linguistic manifestation of a life process."

The Situation and the Supplies

It is my firm conviction that God creates the situation and provides the supplies to share with others the good news. Additional discussion centered on Carl's definition. On close examination, it was good theology for a philosopher who did not believe in God. We discussed this fact at length. Carl's use of the **present tense** initiated an extended dialogue. His **singularity** of one God was interesting. The **possessive or jealous nature** of God with Israel had a good discussion. The fact that God's ways were past finding out centered on Carl's observation about God being the **"abstraction of an adverb."** It was clear that Carl could not understand God as Deity and needed to take small steps into faith.

Function of the Adverb

Carl was a young intellectual and somewhere in his grasp of the use and function of the adverb was the key to an adequate perception of a living and active God. His personal definition would be a beginning; **"An adverb is the linguistic manifestation of a life process."** The God whom Carl defined was not viable to him because there was no systematic order relating the signs and symbols about a Divine Person to his personal reality. In English, an adverb modifies a verb, adjective, or another adverb by expressing time, place, manner, degree, or cause. An adverb also expresses action, existence or occurrence and an adjective expresses a quality, defines or describes a noun. Carl had never witnessed this aspect of the nature of God.

The Action of God

God in this case was the big Noun and Carl had never witnessed the action of God in space and time. He needed someone who had personally experienced the power and action of God to adjust the semantics and syntax of the experience to a language he could accept. Carl needed the same touch of experiential reality that doubting Thomas of scripture desired. Thomas had an opportunity to feel, see, and touch Deity. Carl needed a touch of first hand experiential reality. He needed a manifestation of the resurrected life expressed in one of God's adverbs. At last, the course of action was clear. Carl needed to see one of God's adverbs point to the action of the Big Noun.

God's Adverbs

With this awareness, I altered and repeated the original introduction, **"Good morning, my name is Hollis Green, I am one of God's adverbs."** A spark of cognitive ignition occurred, Carl's mind was open, the heart was ready, and the Holy Spirit had done His work. A simple walk down the Roman Road of scripture brought Carl face to face with the reality of redeeming grace. He accepted not only the present tense existence of the Creator God, but welcomed a personal relationship. Carl became a believer, a fellow adverb to go forth and point to the real time action of God.

Collapse of Organized Religion

When institutions are powerful, the structure normally becomes deaf to criticism. When institutions are weak, designated leadership is usually unable to act upon even constructive criticism. Faith-based groups, as social institutions, are neither as powerful nor as weak as some critics have suggested. Those who see the collapse of organized religion may be irritated because the fall does not happen immediately. It is similar to the "death of God" theology of the past when some critics asked, "If God is dead, why is it taking the clergy so long to bury the cause and probate the estate?" In fact, the leaders of all faith-based groups are immersed in the moral, ethical, legal, social, and economic aspects of their institutions and will not change. The past perspectives restrict human viewpoints and cannot change because of famine, war, or the stroke of a pen. Whether the criticism concerns authority, ineffectiveness, or elitism, little will happen in one generation to make significant change in any social institution. This is part of the problem with the social aspect of organized religion, and their attempts to share their message or propagate their structure to the world.

Several Cultural Influences

Several cultural aspects influence faith-based groups today. Medieval Rome left an authoritative cultural footprint on both society and religion. The Germanic element produced individuality and personal freedom that marks Western culture and influences faith-based groups. The Greek philosophy and language still impacts religion. The original efforts to form the pristine religious groups were primitive and suffered the flaws of polytheistic influence and indigenous cultures that were without simplistic refinement or education. This further complicated a simple expression of the message of grace. As culture complicated communication, the message of grace became multifaceted and misleading. The results were many pretenders who claimed entitlement to positions of honor and few genuine converts and faithful followers.

Entrenchment of Institutions

The entrenchment of institutions causes them to persist long after their usefulness is over. Tradition and custom are as hard to break as a bad habit. With the clergy continually propping up organized religion, the function of the local congregation may become less a spiritual force, and more of a civil or moral conscience to society.   This ability to influence is not all bad.   What is tragic is too lose the foundation and cultural reality that made the group "Messiah-like" in the first place. Some things may never change; other things must change. The one certainty in the modern age is change and change brings anxiety and stress.

Anxiety and Distress

Spiritual hypochondria include anxiety and distress about the wellbeing and viability of faith-based groups and the spiritual illnesses suffered by local congregations and individual faith-based followers. Negative participation by much of the membership has not affected their programs.

Past discussion, concerning the declining influence of the church has been fruitless. The futility of the facts seems to depress leadership and efforts to force participation does not work. Most would rather look to building new and larger buildings, missionary issues, charity for the poor, world famine, or crime directed toward minorities than deal with the real problems facing the individual and the family.

Skepticism or Resistance

Faith-based groups have developed a distinctive form of skepticism or resistance to following sacred injunctions. Elected members of government take an oath to support and defend the basic founding principles and to bear true faith and allegiance to the same. Then there is a clause, "I take this obligation freely, without any mental reservation or purpose of evasion.....So help me God!" If a secular and civil society can require such commitment, why are faith-based groups so tolerant of the violation of founding principles of faith? Why do individuals join a faith group and then not live up to the basic standards of behavior? This failure of modern faith is so detrimental to spiritual and moral progress. Faith-based communications will fail unless there is drastic change in both the attitude and action of people of faith. Freeze frame thinking must be thawed by the true fires of faith.

CHAPTER SIX

DEFROST
FREEZE FRAME THINKING

Searching for classics of the past in an Oxford, England used bookstore, seven (7) selected books were presented to the gray haired gentleman at the counter. I was surprised, even shocked by his questions and comment. He asked, "Are you an American?" My answer was in the affirmative. He then asked, "Are you a member of the cloth?" Declaring myself a member of the clergy, I thought perhaps he was giving me a discount. Then the man petitioned, "Please don't take these books to America. They have already emptied the churches in England!" Out of respect for his wisdom and sincerity, I left the books on the counter and walked out into the cold air of reality. The systematic writings of another culture and time would no longer be considered an acceptable analysis of the Word of God; in the future, I would concentrate on the original intent of scripture based on an understanding of the primary language of the New Testament. This decision removed an academic and traditional obstacle from my understanding of theology.

Grateful for Insight and Wisdom

Grateful for the English gentlemen's insight and wisdom, since that time I have been cautious about picking anything out of another language, culture, or time period and expecting it to work adequately in another culture or community. Faith-based leaders should take caution in copying the programs, plans and policies from other cultures and generations. Scriptural principles remain the same, but each culture must carefully present the good news in the language and social context of the people they wish to reach. Consequently, I spent 42 years of my academic life translating New Testament Greek into a common/devotional language in an attempt to arrive at the original intent of words and how they could best be expressed to the English speaking world. *

_____

*[This 42-year project was published (2012) as The EVERGREEN Devotional New Testament – Complete Edition. See www.gea-books.com and other sites where good books are sold.]

Freeze Frame Faith

The effort to construct a coherent system of belief and practice is rooted in a particular culture and time. Faith-based scholars seemed to stop the action of the theological clock at a particular time in history. The present guidelines for study based on past writings of theologians that produced a freeze frame theology did not have specific relevance to the present. The concepts and constructs from a past cultural context did not adequately inform present theological study. Lifting concepts and constructs from another era and placing them into the complex and multicultural scene of the present no longer made sense. This together with other compounding factors raised barricades to faith-based communication and viability.

A Cinematographic Technique

Some theologians have adopted a cinematographic technique used in sports known as "freeze frame" to stop the action in order to determine the right and wrong of a specific call of a referee. Looking at the freeze frame, an objective observer may affirm a call or rectify a wrong decision. It appears that some have stopped the theological clock at a particular period in history and developed a dogma based on that particular frame of reference. The freeze frame thinking was to affirm an ideology or a particular point of view and pass it on to faith-based groups as the absolute truth. An ideology expresses ideas and values and consists of theology and philosophy together with personal experience. Dogma is a system of principles about faith and behavior established through a systematic study of the scripture plus sacred writings of the past.   This produces a statement of belief preserved from the past and placed in the present culture. It is at this conceptual level that freeze frame thinking constructs multiple theological positions. There seems to be no single edifying voice that lays down the unifying parameters of faith. Consequently, *One Lord, One Faith, One Baptism* has become several sectarian voices competing for a constituency.

The Cause of Most Divisions

This freeze frame thinking about faith and behavior is the cause of most divisions in faith-based groups and change must happen to assure a viable message of grace. Spiritual renewal comes when an individual or a group initiates an effort to dissolve freeze frame thinking and begins to explain scriptural truth in the context of the current needs of the community. This requires both sound judgment, based on a fundamental understanding of sacred scripture, and a realistic grasp of local culture. A practical application of cardinal faith and worship will declare the worth and value of God in all aspects of life. Worship is a vertical experience between an individual and God and differs significantly from human friendship and social fellowship. An experiential reality also differs from an intellectual apprehension of truth.

Linkage between Behavior and Theology

Faith-based groups must establish an adequate relational theology for the present generation to be interested in religion. Almost no effort to defend or plead for a more practical approach to the reality of theological interpretation is self-evident within the faith-based community. The neglect to contextualize an application of scriptural teachings to behavior is a weighty difficulty. There is almost no effort made by religious leaders for a more practical approach to the interpretation of biblical writings.

Legalistic standards exist in some areas, with no realistic application of sacred literature to personal behavior and culture. As a young man speaking to a group of West Virginia miners, using Psalm 23, the miners had no concept of sheep or shepherd. Finally it was determined the Psalm should be interpreted in the context of their local culture. Instead of using the words "...though I walk through the valley of the shadow of death, I will fear no evil: for thou art with me:" Since the Fire Boss of the mines would go into the shaft before a shift to check the general safety of the mine, I decided to apply this to the Psalm. Now, the words were "the Fire Boss goes before me to make the mine safe..." and they clearly understood the Psalm.

The concept of God Incarnate should prompt scholars to make linkage between human behavior and scripture, but the persistent effort is to organize teachings based on the thoughts and opinions of past generations. This produces a systematic rather than a relational theology.

The Idea of Theology

The word "theology" itself is the combination of *theos* (god) with *logos* (word). The idea of theology did not originate with Christians. Historically it entered the scene when the Greeks attempted to develop a synthesis of the myths of the Olympian deities with prehistoric myths. Later theology assumed a philosophic form and became either a rational expression of myth or an abandonment of myth and identification with the metaphysics of being. Through the impact of Greek theoretical thinking, theology entered Judaism and Christianity. The Jewish tradition has resisted the idea of theology, while some cultures such as the Oriental have no concept of theology. Without an understanding of God from either a Greek or a biblical perspective one does not construct an adequate relational theology.

Living Epistles

Some tried to combine biblical tradition and Greek philosophy into a theology, but it did not work. Looking over Paul's shoulder into the written words, it is almost impossible to get into his head and heart, or reproduce the circumstance and atmosphere in which the hearer received Paul's writings. The reality of the Word of God is clear: the Word became incarnate and lived among men. Since the words of scripture are in some abstract or historical form rather than the living language of the people, such words do not communicate the genuine message of grace. Paul suggested that believers were living epistles open and read by others. Remember, early believers did not possess a copy of the New Testament, there were only a few scattered letters read once to a congregation and passed to another group. The people were the vehicle that transported the message; in fact, the medium was the message. The believers had a relationship with the Divine and a genuine fellowship with others, together with enthusiasm to share the blessings of redemptive grace and a hopeful future by lip and life.

A Constructive Method

Theology that is systematically constructed strives toward a complete, philosophic, and a systematic statement of the comprehensive content of theological knowledge. It is a discussion about God based on the compiled information from all the written text on the subject. It includes both the biases of selection and elaboration. This is not to say that a more exegetical theology would be less bias, it is not. This is part of the problem, the collection of sacred writings known as the New Testament, as well as the words, thoughts, and opinions of others about scripture, are selected and expounded upon based on a personal orientation or sectarian prospective of the interpreter. The objective should be to determine what the original language meant "then" and how can the original intent be expressed "now" in a common language.

Scholarship Requires Methodical Study

Scholarship requires that any organized and methodical study of theology presents the facts and permit the reader to make a judgment about the meaning and value of the information. This is not so in any division of theology. A theological treatise is often a "position paper" slanted to defend the author's sectarian position. In other words, it is not an effort to inform or interpret, but an attempt to persuade another to a particular point of view. Through the years, this approach to biblical explanation and interpretation has become a kind of freeze frame theology where ideas, concepts, and representations from the past and presented to support a present position. This subjective approach can never fully satisfy the needs of the faith-groups. The words must have a firm connection to the original language of scripture and be expressed in a present vernacular to be fully understood and accepted by the people.

A More Relevant Theology

Some scholars have called for a more relevant theology that looks ahead and moves forward. The faith-based movement has always been an extension of the horizontal present moving to meet the contemporary needs of people. With the Incarnation, God intended the plan of redemption to meet the human family at the relational level of need. Faith-based groups have always functioned in the secular historic present looking more to the present needs and future state of individuals, rather than looking back. The overwhelming message of the Letter to the Hebrews in Rome was a strong appeal to go forward and never go back to an old system that fulfilled the task of bringing people forward until there was a better way to full redemtion.

Individuals not Institutions

Historians have attempted to make religion more powerful and more influential on the affairs of state, when in reality the institution itself was not the direct influence it was the behavior of believers. The fundamental nature of faith changed the lives of individuals and these committed persons through their lifestyle and decisions influenced the state. What is often lost in the large view of history is the value of the individual and the impact that one good person made on a cause. Sometimes such individuals were known as martyrs, at other times simply forgotten or disregarded in an effort to honor some leader. When in reality no officer ever won a battle and no army ever defeated an enemy; it was the skill and bravery of individual soldiers that produced the victory through painstaking and determined opposition to the enemy. It is individuals who change and individuals who bring about the change in others.

Wrong Message Sent

History gave too much credit to the institution rather than the effect of a changed life on society. By making it appear that religion was doing the good rather than the individual witness, the wrong message was sent to the next generation. Great effort to construct organized religion rather than incarnate faith in the heart and souls of the people. Those called to share the message of grace are often lost in the wilderness of history trying to learn the way it worked in the past so they could replicate the process. This process blinds them from seeing the current needs of the people and using the tenets of faith and the assistance of the Holy Spirit to serve others at their point of need. Time would be better spent to look at the present needs of the people and find creative ways to change personal behavior. This would enable the larger groups, the family units, the community, the small faith-based gatherings, and society to be more moral and ethical and to acknowledge that only God is able to intervene in the global affairs of humanity.

Holy Spirit Transcends Culture

Only the Holy Spirit can transcend the culture of the ages and adequately illuminate the sacred scripture for those who would minister to the secular mind. Certainly, there are no private interpretations of scripture, but the Spirit does make direct application of spiritual truth to the hearts and lives of believers within the context of culture and language. An atmosphere conducive to the objective understanding of preserved scripture comes only with the illumination of the Holy Spirit. This would permit sincere believers to view the Word without scholarly interference. Anything less simply adds to the dilemma. The Word of God does not make sense to the natural man; there must be the clarification of the Spirit. Perhaps, at this point, the Word would work effectively with a cultural specific message to the spiritual ear of the heart.

> 9. Written in scripture, eye has not seen, nor ear heard, neither has entered into the heart of man, the things that God has prepared for those who love Him. 10. But God has unveiled them to us by His Spirit: for the Spirit searches all things, and affirms the deep things of God. 11. For what human being can know the thoughts of a man, save the spirit of man which is in him? Even so no man knows the things of God, but the Spirit of God. 12. We have not received the spirit of the world, but the Spirit that is of God; that we might know the things that are freely given to us by God. 13. We do not speak of these things in language

taught by men, but that which the Holy Spirit teaches; explaining spiritual things in spiritual words. 14. **The natural man does not accept the things of the Spirit of God: for they are nonsense to him: they just do not make sense to him: neither can he understand them, because they are only discerned spiritually.** *(1 Corinthians 2:9-14 EDNT)*

Things are Hard to Understand

The instructive writings of Paul did not assume a systematic form; his words were relational. The unconverted had little chance of understanding the constructs of Paul. It was interpreted in the light of existing culture, but the hearer did not fully understand. The full effect of culture is never completely understood and this affects the interpretation of words. Some doubt the sacred scripture can be understood apart from the culture in which it was first given, but surely there is a way through the maze. The Word of God means exactly what it meant to the first person who heard it. How can we then understand? Peter wrote to believers that some of Paul's writings were hard to understand.

15. Look upon our Lord's longsuffering as salvation; even as our beloved brother Paul has written according to the wisdom given to him; 16. also in all his letters, when he touches on these subjects, **some things are hard to understand, things which those who lack knowledge and a firm foundation in the faith twist, as they do other scriptures, to their own destruction.** *17. For yourselves, beloved, be warned in time; do not be carried away by their impulsive errors, and lose the firm foothold you have won; 18. But grow up in grace, and in the knowledge of our Lord and Savior Jesus Christ. To Him be glory; now and for all eternity. Amen. (2 Peter 3:15-18 EDNT)*

No Religious Vacuum

Renewal and vitality are possible. The present multicultural, evil and polytheistic world is similar to the circumstance that birthed the pristine faith-based groups. Christianity did not begin in a religious vacuum. The human race was not lacking words to believe. The new faith had to fight against entrenched religious traditions and cultural constructs that had existed for centuries. Most of the religious beliefs had degenerated into feeble superstitions and meaningless rituals; others seemed to be new and vigorous. The ancient condition almost describes the present condition of local congregations and faith-based groups in many `countries. In addition to freeze frame theology, the local congregation suffers from top down programming and the effort to bring about sameness. The expression of faith may be as different as the ethnicity and culture of the people. The influence of both constructs from the past and programming that imposes a franchise mindset must diminish for the faith-based message of grace to be viable. Depending on programs sent down from a sectarian source weakens personal involvement in sharing the message of grace. Over dependency on top down programming must diminish for local efforts to flourish.

CHAPTER SEVEN

DIMINISH TOP DOWN PROGRAMMING

A top down strategy in programming is the imposition of a hierarchical structure for local units of a franchise. Such structure is a control mechanism used in organizations to maintain sameness of operations. Life experience teaches that each individual is different, each group has different perspectives, and each community has cultural and traditional differences; consequently, programs that are one size fits all will not work everywhere. When this approach is used for faith-based groups, creativity and personal initiative are stifled. To be viable as a spiritual and positive social change agent in a community, a local congregation must diminish top down influence and tailor local programs to the needs of the community. One should never throw out the baby with the bath water, but diminishing top down programming is a good strategy.

A Newsprint Picture of a Skunk

Traveling to Washington, D.C., during the Vietnam War to intercede for a young service man mistreated because of his faith, God opened a door for me to witness. Just before catching the plane, my schedule took me to a publisher to review the galley proof of a book. An old newspaper was on the floor. Since neatness is a virtue, my decision was to pick up the paper. It was stuck to the floor and covering an ink spill. In the process of picking up the newsprint, a small piece tore off in my hand. It was a picture of a skunk and a story about a farmer.

An Abandoned Home

A Pennsylvania farmer had observed an old skunk for several days. One day the skunk abandoned his old home and dug a fresh nesting hole. The farmer was intrigued, so he watched. The skunk with great care gathered grass and leaves and lined the inside of the excavation. The skunk looked around for what was to be his last glance at the world, and then entered his final resting place. The behavior fascinated the farmer so he waited. When the skunk never came out of the hole, the farmer became curious. What was the lesson learned?

God Had a Reason

Taking a stick, the farmer punched into the hole, but nothing happened. Finally, he knelt down and raked back the leaves so he could see the skunk. The skunk did not move; it was dead. The farmer observed that the skunk was old, the teeth were broken, and concluded the skunk could no longer hunt for food and had prepared to die. Reading this story seemed foolish at the time, but God had a reason. There was a lesson learned that was to be pasted to a young soldier on his way to Vietnam.

The Empty Seat

Seated about half way back in the coach section, a young soldier chose the empty seat beside me. As the plane took off, the soldier turned and said, "Sir, I probably won't be alive a year from now; I'm on my way to Vietnam." This matter of fact statement jolted my memory of the skunk story. Sharing the story with the young soldier, his face became thoughtful. The time had come for me to present the claims of faith. If an old skunk had enough sense to prepare to die, surely it would be wise for a soldier going to battle to prepare to die.

Prepared to Die

The young soldier's answer, "Sir, I would if I knew how." The door was wide open, and the ABC's of the gospel (**A**ll have sinned, **B**elieve on the Jesus Christ, and **C**onfess with your mouth the Lord Jesus, and you will be saved) were presented. The young soldier prayed to receive and went to war prepared to die. God used a book manuscript, spilled ink, an old newspaper story about a skunk, and a plane ride to assist a soldier persecuted for his faith, and a troubled and searching heart, to do the work of redemption for a young soldier. I often thought about that young man. Perhaps his name is on the Vietnam Memorial Wall, but I do not know his name. One thing is certain: his name is in the Lamb's Book of Life. Perhaps I will see him again on the other side of Jordan.

A Philosophy of Ministry

Interviewing pastors about a philosophy of ministry, some answers shocked me. "I really don't have a philosophy, I just wait on Sunday." Another answer about daily prayer, "If I do all the programs send down from headquarters, I don't have time to pray." A seminarian responded about his chosen place for ordination. "I really haven't made a choice. I am not physically able to handle all the programs sent down from the organization to local churches and still have energy to do my ministry calling. I am searching for a group that will permit me to have an active community ministry rather than just manage generic programs sent to all the churches. Each community is different and I want to use my energies for things that work where God puts me." This young man wanted to bloom where God planted without the encumbrance of unrealistic expectations of top down programs.

A Matter of Choice

The membership of faith-based groups should embrace the principles that undergird their faith as their own. It is a matter of choice, but often the leadership or the members of local congregations do not make the choice to follow clear principles. Many are reluctant to accept the generalization that scripture is truth, nor is the essence of the faith a basis for reasoning or conduct. Religious leaders should remember that the failed philosophy of Communism was "The end justifies the means." Just because a process or procedure worked for the moment does not mean it is good for the future needs of the people over time.

Principle vs. Pragmatism

The functional criterion should be principle before pragmatism. The criteria of scriptural teachings should be the driving force in a faith-based lifestyle, not a marketing survey or a top down program. Pragmatism has triumphed over principle repeatedly as religious leaders look to public opinion and sectarian guidance in making decisions. Form and function works together to facilitate positive change, but methodology alone cannot transform a gathering of strangers into a community of saints. God uses human beings as both the medium and the message to share the message of grace. The programmatic approach to faith-based missionary outreach is a sacrilege. Certainly, a place of worship is a social institution operated by people; therefore, the human factor should be part of faith-based planning.

The Practical Imperatives

People follow faith-based practices they see validated by the changing of lives. What works should influence decisions to share the message of grace based on scriptural standards, or the true cause of pristine faith is in jeopardy. Consequently, one should not judge an assembly by attendance, but by the character of the participants. Quality counts! The quantity of participation is only important when the standards undergirding the behavior of members are adequately measured. If faith-based groups are to stem the tide of secularization, principles must guide and become the practical imperatives.

Scriptural and Needed

Coming together to worship is both scriptural and needed to encourage, edify, and equip the Family of God to function adequately within contemporary society. This does not alter the need for the development of a moral lifestyle by individual believers. Now, more than ever, the faith-based groups need to reach deeply into the foundations of faith-base heritage and develop a corporate worship and an individual lifestyle based on spiritual principles.

Principles Enhanced by Divine Encounter

Sectarian models, with a franchised program, are not the way to base the operation of faith-based congregations on principles. Operating from an ethical base rather than historic models is the answer. The early faith-based believers of history did not have models, just basic principles enhanced by a divine encounter and genuine commitment. The context of each local fellowship was different and the message of grace applied to the culture and language of the community.

Develop a Functional Implementation

The practice of pragmatism must not determine the criteria for spiritual knowledge or the operational definitions for spiritual principles and values. Faith-based groups must develop a functional implementation of the common faith heritage validated by a fresh search for the relevant meaning of words as they apply to the present generation. Such functionality requires scriptural principles and expression compatible with the culture of the local community. It requires a harmonious mixture of race, culture and ethnicity in the community and standardized with the scriptural message of grace for the present generation. Faith-based leadership must guard against arbitrary changes that encroach on the essential elements of faith-based lifestyles.

Heritage worth Remembering

The Reformers personally embraced the essence of faith and applied the real meaning to their lives. It worked for a while, until various theologians began to interpret in writing their personal views as to the meaning of scripture. These personal views were imposed on faith-based groups through systematic theological study. Now believers must abandon most past interpretations of scripture and return to the basics of personal faith otherwise they will be lost in the corporate structure and institutional explanation of scripture. This has become spiritual manipulation rather than experiential faith based on a spiritual illumination of sacred scripture. The practices handed down from the Reformers are a heritage worth remembering, but just as modern man does not use a horse and buggy or cross the ocean in a sailing ship, many of the theological concepts constructed in the past are not relevant to current living. Past generations did have a message for the present generation, but that message was not preserved in a useable form for the present. The meaning of words change; therefore, one must return to the original scriptural language to determine the true meaning of the word "then" and find the best way to express the meaning "now" in the present culture. There is great value in the principles they used to deal with the cultural relevance of words, but the process is different because the meanings of words have changed in the following centuries. Each generation has specific problems that must have fresh solutions. This is true in a faith-based life.

House Church vs. Cathedral

There are no universal models. The constant experimentation with the structural practicalities of the local worship and witness has broken the linkage with the historic past. The spiritual memory has been lost and words are used for which there is no relevant meaning. This has confused the sense of mission and muddled the message of grace. The humble house church led by the father as priest of the family that glorified sacred truth during the New Testament era became a secular cathedral led by a professional staff with little lay involvement. This overvalues the spiritual leadership of humans at the expense of true redemption by the hand of God. Without a spiritual anchor in a raging sea of social change, the identity and function of individuals are confused. Action based on scriptural principles and genuine concern for people is the only answer to the decline seen in local congregations and the only hope for constructive social change. The local outreach agenda handed down must be disassembled and replaced by a simple people-to-people plan that operates with a fresh and enthusiastic witness of personal faith.

CHAPTER EIGHT

RESIST
GOVERNMENTAL CONTROL

Antidisestablishmentarianism is a long English word that actually has meaning. Depending on the dictionary used, it means "opposition to the withdrawal of state support or recognition from an established church." In other words, once a state recognizes a religion, there is legal opposition to ending this authorization. This is one major reason for resisting governmental control of religion and faith-based activities.

Some nations have a state church or an official religion and assume some oversight and control of functions, teachings, or organizational matters. Many modern countries recognize the Roman Catholic Church as a state religion. When a state recognizes a Christian church the term *state church* is used, but other religions such as Islam, Buddhism, and Hindu have state religions. Israel is a Democratic Jewish State. Further control over religion is exercised through the *state church*; such as, the Church of Greece, Finnish Orthodox Church, Church of Denmark, Church of Iceland, Church of Norway, Evangelical Lutheran Church of Finland, Church of Ireland, Church of Scotland, and of course the Church of England. This is only a few; there are many others. It is difficult enough when human beings control a religious organization, but this pales in comparison to the state control of religion. Under all circumstances, believers must resist governmental control. Would it not be wonderful if faith-based groups could fully return the helm of the Old Gospel Ship to the true Captain?

Audacity and Spiritual Courage

During the build up to WWII, Hitler and the Third
Reich in their opposition to Judaism attempted to control
all religions and bring the German church under Nazi
supervision. Dietrich Bonhoeffer faced death in a Nazi
prison because of his personal courage by resisting
governmental control of the German church. His personal
resistance to Hitler's effort to control the church initiated the
process that led to his execution. Through the Confessing
Church, which resisted governmental infringement,
Bonhoeffer began to develop the concepts of principled
responsibility in relation to the spiritual life. During his
imprisonment, he worked further on a personalized
approach to discipleship.

Bonhoeffer expressed a different perspective on
life and religion in his prison letters to Eberhard Bethge, a
trusted friend. It took real courage to live the disciplined
life during wartime, but perhaps it takes more audacity and
spiritual courage to resist secular control of the faith-based
community in times of peace. Silently, civil government
has encroached on the nature of marriage, abortion
issues, and the subject of death and dying. Recently, the
state attempted to impose governmental control over
some matters of conscience that have been the purview
of religious institutions for centuries. The faith-based
community must resist all encroachment.

An Antecedent Obligation

Although Bonhoeffer made fragmentary suggestions
about a time when there would be no religion at all, his
statements concerned the reality of faith, not the formal,
public expression of religion. He believed that religion
had an antecedent obligation that binds believers as a
social force to certain responsibility. He suggested that the
meanness of war annihilated this viable historical possibility

of religion. Looking at the tragedy of war, Bonhoeffer understood that preaching and teaching of the German church did not create a human conscience to prevent the inhumanity of armed conflict during the decades of two world wars. The armed conflict crushed the internal principles by which Germany engaged the world and the men who committed wartime atrocities had been under the influence of the German church for decades. The tragedy, according to Bonhoeffer, was that the church seemed to have no influence on the social policies of the government or the behavior of the German soldier.

Religion without old Presuppositions

Bonhoeffer in his earliest mention of a new "religion-less world" (30 April 1944) suggested that men in the future would speak of God in a secular manner rather than as theologians. He not only raised the possibility of different means of expressing religious language, but that it would be without the old presuppositions and institutional aspects of the *state church*. He pointed to a time when believers would return to the individual level of faith and practice based on biblical principles rather than the institutionalized format that persists in Western culture. This is the basic proposition of this book.

Perhaps organized religion will be permitted to continue its crippled performance of playing church, the second front of missionary outreach will be allowed to waste vital resources through defective efforts, and the ineffective guerilla-type operation of unprepared individuals functioning on foreign soil, digging wells, planting corn, and teaching carpentry, will be lauded as a religious "peace corps." This happening while the streets of the work-a-day world and the marketplace of ideas and values are completely lacking the true influence of grace.

An Adulterated Religiosity

Bonhoeffer's letters pointed to a confidence that "religion" was to be and should be an expression of personal godliness rather than the teachings of an organized religion. His writings suggested that the nurturing of the institutional church would not complete an individual's life. This fulfillment comes only by the addition of God to life through a personal divine encounter. Such an experience could make a difference in the behavior of those who were truly submerged in a faith-based lifestyle. This concept conflicts with the pragmatism of modern religious philosophy that attempts to manage and manipulate human behavior. Such efforts fail to understand the historical reality of the human race. The effort to manipulate does not produce a different person, because the teachings degenerate into a kind of secular religion. Such behavior produces a fatherless fantasy, an adulterated religiosity, and an immoral society.

The human race is not free of past religious influence. Modern ideologies have expressed and extended their hold on the population through the institutionalization of religion. The concept that "man had learned to cope with important questions without recourse to God as a working hypothesis" when written it was Bonhoeffer's original idea (8 June 1944). This concept troubled Bonhoeffer during the final days before his execution at the hands of the Gestapo. He struggled with poetry and letters in a rush to leave a legacy for German believers.

A More Personalized Lifestyle

One day following devotions using Numbers 11:23 and 2 Corinthians 1:20, Bonhoeffer wrote about the promise God gave Moses concerning Divine deliverance. In this devotional mode, he wrote, (21 August 1944) about the believer's "final Amen" and made an appeal for personal Christianity. He postulated that believers must repeatedly immerse themselves in the "life, sayings, deeds, suffering and death of Jesus, to know what God promises and fulfills... again in these turbulent times we lose sight of why it is really worth living." Had he survived the war, many believed he would have continued this effort to redirect German believers toward a more personalized lifestyle of religious devotion and witness.

A Rush to Leave a Legacy

Time is short; the days of man are numbered. The circumstance of life constrain men to hand down to the remaining generations a legacy of achievement. There is little time to leave such a legacy. The average lifespan for men is 78 years and for women is 81 years. Jesus was only 33. Martin Luther King was 39. JFK was 46. Napoleon was 51. The time and manner of death is not in the hand of individuals, but the legacy to others is firmly in both hands as a gift to the beneficiaries.

Before Dietrich Bonhoeffer walked out of the concentration camp barracks for the last time, he whispered to a fellow prisoner, "This is the end; for me, the beginning of life." Bonhoeffer, stripped naked, died on a hangman's gallows on the cold morning of April 9, 1945. He was only 39 years old, yet his legacy lives and Germany and the world benefited from his life. His legacy still speaks volumes to those who will listen and follow his example of commitment to a faith-based lifestyle regardless of the cost of discipleship. The end was worth the journey.

Discipleship and Ethics

Individuals, following the example of Bonhoeffer and others, must attack the evils of the present society that threaten the integrity of the faith-based community. The challenge of Bonhoeffer's life and practical theology deals with discipleship and ethics and speaks directly to the present needs of the human race. A willingness to take risks that come from a devotional and principled heart is necessary to capture the spirit of Bonhoeffer. His writings could provide faith-based leadership a new perspective about worship and personal lifestyle behavior.

Principles from Scripture

A process or procedures based only on the heritage and writings of the past may not be sufficient; the action should be based on the pristine principles of sacred scripture with a fresh understanding of biblical language and the true meaning of words. The Word of God means exactly and only what the first hearer understood it to mean, not what historical commentaries interpret it to mean. A fresh look at the New Covenant would affirm the words still retain their authentic meaning.   This is the only way to deal with the present problems in a significant and consequential way. A predisposition to act responsibly and timely to resist the evil of structures that impinge on the freedom of individuals and local congregations should be part of the effort that drives the present need for change. Sectarian restraints conflict with the present need to advance beyond the usual limits of religious reformation.

True believers must resist the infringement of a secular society and civil government into the affairs of religion and personal faith. Direction for personal behavior must come from the sacred scripture and the guidance of the Holy Spirit. Three relevant examples for faith-based behavior: (1) These words of First Century disciples, "We must obey God rather than man" could be a guide to faith-based behavior. (2) Polycarp, a Second Century Bishop's final words "He who grants me to endure the fire will enable me also to remain on the pyre unmoved, without the security you desire from nails." (3) Saeed Abedini, an American pastor arrested (2012), and imprisoned because his faith threatened the national security of Iran. In a letter to his wife, Abedini affirmed that persecution would never cause him to deny Christ.

A Trustworthy Foundation

The present generation must have spiritual renewal. A clear understanding of the original intent of words in the original language can produce a true spiritual heritage. The precise words of sacred scripture alone should guide renewal and lifestyle, with a minimum of cultural and traditional interference. Leaders should take hold of current issues and deal from personal convictions to cause needed change. Surely, the corporate structure of organized religion cannot produce meaningful change to meet the spiritual needs of the present generation without a sure scriptural foundation. There must be a better way. The answer is basic, personalized spiritual experience with a sacred appreciation for historical roots and heritage without using these as a guide. Validated and trustworthy scripture must be the authority that controls the process of spiritual renewal.

Walking a Treadmill

Entrenched leaders, regardless of how or why they arrived at their position of authority, often develop a personal stake, which further complicates the involvement of others. Leaders become comfortable with the way things happen for their convenience. This becomes an entitled benefit and a major obstacle to advancing the message of grace. Such leaders appear to be walking a religious treadmill. Caught in a prison of previous pattern, there is a great deal of motion without progress. The staff is hyperactive, but the congregation is passive and sleeps like a giant. Faith-based groups have developed an active shepherd--passive sheep structure with little hope of significant change. Most faith-based groups have adjusted their worship and lifestyle to mediocrity and settled for something less than true spirituality. A congregation is not supposed to be a hospital for saints or a social club for sinners; in reality, the place of worship is to be a house of prayer and a mission of faith with lifestyle support for outreach to the community. When faith-based groups neglect outreach to a local community, they fail to be a band of believers and are unable to share the message of grace. The dependency on religious buildings as a sanctuary of the sacred becomes a structured failure.

CHAPTER NINE

DECREASE DEPENDENCY ON BUILDINGS

Major growth of the monotheistic movement in Africa, Asia, and Latin America shows that Africa has the largest concentration of adherents. What does this mean for a faith-based community that has been associated primarily with the culture of Europe and America for centuries? Perhaps the area of growth, being in the less developed countries, speaks to the limited value of highly developed programs and formal specialized buildings as fixed places for worship.

Specialized Buildings Limit Outreach

Specialized buildings, as fixed places for the gathering of believers, did not exist until over 100 years after the death of Christ. Prior to this, believers worshipped in available synagogues and gathered for prayer and fellowship in homes. When a fixed building became a place to worship, the home meetings gave way to a regular assembly in a specialized building. It is not possible to tear down all the houses of worship, but the structured barrier that keeps believers "inside" a building also limits the use of their "outside voice" in the community.

Notwithstanding the benefits of a dedicated structure, building dependency limits outreach. Tragically, the construction and maintenance of these buildings come from thousands of voluntary contributions considered an expression of devotion to the faith. These sacrificial gifts contribute little to the advancement of the faith-based group. The cost of operating the organization further limits the opportunity for outreach.

Change may come in this process when followers become aware of personal responsibility for advancing the faith. Only when congregants personally face their mortality and realize that time is limited for personal participation, will they become active in the advancement of the faith. Followers will become leaders and active witnesses "as they go" only when they realize people are the church, not the buildings or the activities within the structure. Believers must work outside the four walls to become "salt" and "light" as living epistles in the community with the message of grace.

A Place Called "Church"

Overtime the gathering of family and friends for prayer and fellowship become known as church. How did this happen? The scholars commissioned to produce the King James Bible received specific instructions that the word "church" must not be translated "congregation" or any other similar rendering of the original language. The term *synagogue* obviously meant "assembly" and was a gathering of Jewish worshippers. The Greeks used the term *ekklesia* to identify "the assembly of citizens" and this assembly was a "congregation." By 1600 AD, the term "church," was in common use in England for a building and not as a gathering of people.   Consequently, the King James translators were given fifteen general rules as guidance including Rule # 3 about the word "church."

"General Rule # 3

The clear intent of Rule # 3 was to establish the term "church" as a building. *"The Old Ecclesiastical words to be kept, viz. the word Church not to be translated Congregation."* Why was this instruction included in the guidelines for the translators? The official Church of England wanted to establish "church" as a building, not as a congregation of people. It was to their advantage for the translators to ignore all the possible rendering of the word; such as, assembly, congregation, meeting, gathering, fellowship, and assist in firmly establishing the structure as the fixed identity of the church rather than the collective band of believers.

Church is not a Building

This book does not use the word "church" to mean a building for public worship connected to a sectarian group. It is used as a broad term for believers joined together to advance a moral or religious cause; that is, an assembly, a community of faith, a congregation, a spiritual fellowship, a gathered group, a band of believers, the flock of God or any organization or group intentionally connected to a faith-based cause. The English term "church" in its cognate forms, *kirche, kerk, kirk,* comes from the Greek adjective, *kuriakon,* meaning "belonging to the Lord." The understanding was a gathering of the people belonging to the Lord. The common Greek word *ekklesia* normally translated as "church" was used in Acts 19:32-41 to clearly represented an assembly of people in a large capacity theatre. The theatre was a place, but the assembly was a gathering of people. When the term church lost this significance, it became a liability to a faith-based advance.

All places where the faithful gather for prayer and fellowship may be considered "belonging to the Lord." Gradually, places where worshippers gathered became buildings instead of an assembly of believers. Lost in this concept of "church" was that the band of believers were the people of God when they were scattered in the community as well as when they gathered in a sanctuary for protection, prayer, and fellowship. This was as true as sheep were a "flock" in the pastureland and in the sheepfold!

Places of Worship

The places of worship have many names: synagogue, temple, church, chapel, tabernacle, or mosques, but all are a gathering of the faithful. Church then is people not a building; when they are "gathered" together as believers they sing, pray, worship, and fellowship. "Church" is also people when they are "scattered" in the community, in the marketplace, in the streets, and in the homes. Their work is more than religious services; it is "disciple making" as they go about their daily lives. The gathering place may function for baptism and instructions in spiritual matters, but the "church" is people not a building. Dependency on buildings must decrease and a stronger emphasis placed on the ministry of the people in the community.

Believers Thrived without Buildings

The personal faith of early believers thrived in the days before specifically constructed buildings became places of worship. Persecution drove early followers of Jesus into homes for prayer and protection. Perhaps this is how the home became a gathering place known as a sanctuary. With pillows to cushion the floor and walls for protection, the house of prayer became a gathering of family and friends. As believers become at ease in a home-like place, dependence grew on the building as a safe place to pray, worship, and meditate. Assembling in someone's home brought limits of space and time for religious activities. The home was the family living quarters and gradually the gathered times for prayers and fellowship needed space and a place. The framework of family activities guided the times of meetings, and ultimately suggested an alternative meeting place. This separation compartmentalized and fractured the faith-based witness, with the meeting place holding dominance over religious lifestyle in the community.

Overcompensated by Constructing Buildings

As religion dealt with false teachers, persecution, and scattered believers, it appears some groups overcompensated by constructing buildings and requiring regular attendance. New wine in old bottles in the use of buildings for religious services has become a growing problem for faith-based groups. Religion as a cultural mix creates a confluence of cultures and buildings are static and may send mixed signals. Some in the faith-based community appear to need buildings to maintain both the local effort and the linkage with others. Many view their faith as connectional and become dependent on buildings and fellowship with others of similar faith. This nature of faith as connectional together with the cost of stationary buildings in a migrating and multicultural society creates dependence on buildings and sectarian groups.

Dependency Began

Depending on a safe place to pray and fellowship began to limit the religious activities of the group. During the workday, believers began to share a testimony of faith and encourage others to come to the meeting place. Religious activity became dependent on a place, a building, and meeting times. This began the process of compartmentalizing the lives of the family. Overtime the place of worship became a specialized building no longer used as a home for a family. Since the gathering place was a building, a dependency developed and spiritual activity became evaluated based on attendance at the building at specific times.

Leaders are Co-dependents

The clerics and staff at the gathering place have become co-dependents in the process of supporting the concept that the "church" was a building. They normally have a psychological addiction to the ways and means of constructing the operation of "church." This self-serving function is disguised as ministry to people, yet, their work is almost completely in support of the *status quo*. This has decreased the effectiveness and the efficiency of the spiritual advance in the community.

Behavior of a Single Convert

Spiritual behavior of a single convert sharing with family and friends moved to a group gathering with likeminded folk for fellowship, prayer and reading of scripture. Gradually, some shared on subjects based on scripture readings; while others sang and some testified of God's redemption. Gradually, activities became stereotyped and the routine was a turn off to both members and visitors and negative participation began. Faith-based operation must move back to the home-style, living room sanctuary, with a marketplace ministry where believers can share their faith and lead friends to a knowledge of mercy and the message of grace.

The Power of Tradition

Tradition develops visual expression of religious buildings. A watchtower embodied the aspiration that its name implied. Towers of old churches sent the message of security to the community. A minaret attached to an Islamic mosque is a signal to call the people to prayer. The bell tower is part of parish churches in most English and European communities. Emergent faith-based groups, as an unprotected minority, could not afford to construct or own buildings, so they met in houses and baptized in rivers. As Baptists, Congregationalists, and Quakers were accepted, they built new style religious buildings: meeting houses and chapels. These buildings were not cathedrals, but simple and functional places to gather. Such places would not become shrines. The simplicity of these early buildings with their graveyards reflected the family-life of the people: in life and death, they were a community separated from the general population.

Specific Architecture

The architecture of modern church buildings is specific to faith-based groups and easily recognized. They differ significantly from the old European buildings. There seems to be two main ways of looking at religious buildings: some are mainly shrines that preserves the past for the sightseer, while others are regular meeting places for worship by a local community. People visit a shrine occasionally, but do not attend it regularly. Only a faithful few belong and attempt to maintain the past. There is a different attribution given to a shrine than to a building that houses a regular congregation. How did a gathering of family and friends, become a gathering of strangers? Some elaborate buildings may have contributed to the church buildings becoming a kind of shrine that is honored with only a few infrequent visits.

Phenomenon of the Reformation

The schedule of services has a common origin. The scheduling of early Mass on Sunday morning with only a few seats around the walls was a tradition for years. Many community activities were part of the schedule using parts of the buildings not suitable for worship. The church building was often the only covered place in the community where people could gather for social and civil events. The band of believers survived for centuries without regular services in specific buildings, but gradually became dependent on the scheduled activities.

A phenomenon of the Reformation was that the church building became a place to gather on special days. The forerunner of these services did not come to England until Tudor times. The times (11 AM and 6:30 PM) and length of services were printed in the Book of Common

Prayer (1549). Following this publication, attendance at the stated services became the norm for evaluating religious commitment. The difference of culture and people, notwithstanding, much of the religious tradition around the world is base on these facts.

Dependent on Buildings

The migrating Israelites could pack up their place of worship and move it with them. A Muslim could take his prayer mat along. The Buddhist could make a shrine in his home or yard. Christians on the other hand became dependent on a building and a clergy led program of worship to maintain an active faith. Regardless of the advantages of protection against weather and the ability to shut the world out, faith-oriented buildings became a hindrance to reaching a population who would not attend without an official invitation. The band of believers developed a "come strategy" and access to the message and mission of grace became limited.

Hospital for Saints or Social Club

A gathered band of believers is not supposed to be a hospital for saints or a social club for sinners; in reality, the place of worship is to be a house of prayer and a mission of faith with lifestyle support for outreach to the community. Reliance on religious buildings as the only sanctuary of the sacred has become a liability. Sacred writings are clear: God uses people to advance the mission of grace, not buildings or organized programs. In fact, the facts are evident as to the obsolescence of building-based programs and policies in the age of technology.

An Ounce of Spiritual Enthusiasm

The old adage, "An ounce of prevention is worth a pound of cure," could easily be worded, "An ounce of spiritual enthusiasm is worth thousands of square feet of building." Yet the faith-based hierarchy continues to pour scarce resources into property and programs rather than equipping believers to be priests in the family and witnesses in the marketplace. The facts demonstrate that funds expended on facilities have not proportionally advanced the gospel. Reality demonstrates that a small amount of demonstrated affection and personal attention can make a significant difference in outreach and personal witness in the community.

Message Established in People

People are the facilitators of the message of faith, not property. The objective ought to be confidently assisting individuals in establishing lifestyle witnessing, but construction of buildings continue among a neglected people. Organizations are busy constructing buildings rather than fostering a moral lifestyle among constituents. Buildings, not personal involvement, have become the most planned part of religion, especially, in a society characterized by mobility. Similar structures have replaced many common aspects of personal involvement. The large investment of funds in single use property has become the greatest detriment to advancement of faith in the community.

Departure of a Constituency

Deserted church buildings point to a former presence and the departure of a constituency. These buildings send a message of paradise lost and breed contempt for the faith. Just as great mounds cover the temples of antiquity, the negative aspects of migration and climate change has rescinded the sacred trust and brought disrespect to once dignified places of worship. This reproach has been going on all over the world for most of recorded history. Buildings that survived are used a museums and symbols of the past with little or no relevance to the present. Once worship was a gathering of family and friends, but because of a mobile society religious services have become a gathering of strangers.

Perpetuated the Dependency

Migration brought traditions into new world buildings. The heritage and culture of settlers shaped the buildings. The grandeur of embellished cathedrals as well as the austere simplicity of religious orders influenced small churches and new buildings. Regardless of the background of the people, the forms of worship and the serviceable use of space shaped the religious buildings. The fastest growing groups, such as the Pentecostal and community churches have built modern buildings and are attracting people of the communities who seek to be free from past traditions. Such congregations often down play their sectarian identity with a more generic approach to both building and worship. Sadly, they have perpetuated the dependency on religious buildings.

Spirituality Assessed based on Attendance

Tragically, the assessment of spirituality level based on attendance rather than an active relationship with God has become the norm. An absence from scheduled meetings stimulates a negative response by the group. As one elderly woman declared after missing a few services due to health issues, "The church visitors meant well, but they made me feel like I stole a horse." How can such negativity, coming from a dependence on one's presence in a building, be beneficial to the cause of faith? True worship is a vertical response dealing with the worth and value of God in life expressed in a moral lifestyle. However, most congregations participate more in fellowship than in worship. Faith-based groups must find a better way to instruct believers in a disciplined lifestyle, morality in family life, and personally sharing the message of grace. Perhaps small groups similar to the house churches of the

New Testament could be part of dealing with the present problem.

When Groups Neglect Outreach

When faith-based groups neglect community outreach, the congregation fails to be a band of believers on a quest to share the message of grace. Most would rather look to building new and larger buildings, increase foreign missionary issues, provide charity for the poor, be involved in world famine, or crime directed toward minorities, than deal with the real problems facing the individual and the family. People of faith are best suited to work with local problems. As part of the faith equation, believers have a moral and ethical obligation to influence individuals, families, and society through a message of grace.

Adequate Evidence

History has adequate evidence of persecuted individuals, who were unable to building buildings, but survived and flourished. House-based groups in Mainland China grew surrounded by strong opposition to organized religion by the state. Faith continued at the personal and family level. The record shows that high officials of the defunct USSR returned to organized religion at the demise of the Soviet Union. One high official in the Foreign Office of the USSR accepted baptism the final day of the Union. What does this say about the function of history and the viability of basic faith-based convictions even when maintained without public support?

Seed of Monotheistic Faith

The seeds of monotheistic faith planted in China in the 5th century were slow in growing and eventually sparked overt persecution when Communism assumed governmental control. Yet, in the midst of an evolving communistic culture, the underground churches flourished worshipping in caves, homes, and in the fields. Some estimate that there are at least 30 million monotheistic believers presently in China. Believers were part of unregistered fellowships and functioned as a persecuted minority in mainland China. This was an indigenous phenomenon and many still worship in the underground faith-based groups in China.

The Legacy of Early Witnesses

The legacy of early missionaries is that believers thrived without government recognition and without the conventional buildings. The growth of the underground church, points to the value of seeing the "church" as people scattered in the community rather than thinking the church to be a particular building in a permanent place. Early believers functioned in "house churches," and prospered without formal buildings as a scattered band of believers. The record of the underground church is similar to the early history of Hebrew monotheists:

> 34. Quenched the power of fire, escaped the edge of the sword, in their weakness they were made strong, showed courage in battle, made foreign armies yield. 35. There were women who received their dead children back to life: and others were tortured, not accepting deliverance; looking forward to a better res- urrection: 36. and others experienced mockery and scourging, chains and imprisonment; 37. they were stoned, they were cut in pieces, they were tortured, they were slain with the sword; they wandered about, dressed in animal skins; being destitute, afflicted, tor- mented; 38. men of whom the world was not worthy: they wandered in desert places, and in mountains, and lived in caves and holes in the earth. 39. And these all, having obtained a good report through faith, received not the promise: 40. For us, God had

something better in store. We were needed, to make the history of their lives complete. (Hebrews 11:34-40 EDNT)

"Come to Church!"

Where the "as you go" strategy was tried, it worked better than the "come strategy." The ineffectiveness of "You'll Come" is self-evident. Faith-based groups must make constructive change to reach the current generation. Integrating believers into society to do the personal work of ministry is the last hope for survival for a stagnant faith –based congregation. A good example, is General Booth's project when the state sponsored churches of England were dying a slow and painful death as attendance declined, he initiated the Salvation Army. Defending his efforts, Booth explained the ringing church bells seem to say, "Come to church, come to church" but the people do not come. My army goes to the streets and beats the base drum that says, "Fetch um! Fetch um! And we get them!"

Religious Words to Popular Tunes

Taking the message to the streets and meeting the people at their point of need was faith-based outreach. General Booth understood this fact and the Salvationists stationed outside a busy Pub with the band playing popular tunes extended the message of grace. When the music filtered into the Pub, men would gather to hear the music with Booth's people singing religious words to popular tunes. The salvation message reached the lost, the lonely, and the forgotten. Most would never enter the stately religious buildings. This has been the history of the monotheistic movement.

An "as you go" Strategy

As faith-based groups deserted the "as you go" strategy of the first century, leadership substituted a "come strategy" in an effort to fill empty buildings. Sadly, for generations the common life of faith has been associated with attending a religious service in a building. With the desire to express the common message through the erected edifice, the witness on the street became silent. It appears that some believe religion cannot survive without the shelter of specialized facilities. Others have concluded that inviting prospective converts to the building has not worked effectively. Still others wish to mount a campaign that disperses active members into society to utilize personal contacts one on one and in small groups to share a faith-based message.

CHAPTER TEN

DISASSEMBLE LOCAL OUTREACH AGENDA

A missing link in the outreach agenda is the absence of grass-root participation. Individual members were absent from the decision-making process and program planning. Since an officer does not win a battle without the personal involvement of foot soldiers, outreach programs must have lay involvement to be effective. Personal initiative is essential to advancement. Normally, it is back to square one to disassemble flawed programs and replace them with enthusiastic individuals sharing their faith through an active and moral lifestyle with family and friends. Normally, only those who witness a lifestyle change in others are willing to consider accepting the change that comes with conversion. Individual initiative in lifestyle outreach must replace programs that do not work. Using remotely constructed programs could cause one to abandon personal initiative and influence. Dependence on such advanced packaged program is not compatible with friendship evangelism. Individuals prefer to use tools that fit their hand and personality.

A Surge Protector Named Jesus

Lightning is a massive shock caused by an unbalanced electric charge in the atmosphere that drastically shocks the point of contact. The outreach effort of the faith-based community is drastically unbalanced. It appears that most programs are top down with little initiative from those who must implement the program. When lightning severely disassembled a surge protector in my office without damaging the attached equipment, it taught a worthy lesson. The protector was under warranty but the other items were unable to continue their task. The system protects the top down programmers, but new connections will bring initiative to the people that outsource the message of grace. Explaining that nothing plugged into the protector was hurt, the operator said, "The surge protector did what it was deigned to do, it sacrificed itself for the benefit of the other items." My comment, "When the replacement protector arrives, I will name it Jesus," was met with silence. Obviously, my comment was too religious for a secular society, but it expressed the lesson learned. Perhaps reconnecting the people to the Source and the intermediary be disassembled is the answer.

Institutionalized Weapons

The Hebrew Shepherd Boy could not use the institutionalized weapons of King Saul. Instead, young David used his familiar sling and a smooth brook stone to defeat the giant that terrorized Israel's army. David took the facts of Israel's desperate situation and disassembled the weapons of warfare that would not work for him and used initiative and familiar tools together with the guiding hand of God to win the battle against the giant. The shepherd lad could not fight Goliath in the armor of King Saul. The sophisticated weapons of the monarch were not suitable for his personal use. Tools must always fit the hand of the user to insure a good outcome. David also anticipated the next step and selected five stones because Goliath had four brothers. David not only used personal initiative and refused to fight with weaponry structured by others, he used a handmade tool and with God's assistance won the battle. All workers must be willing participants in the process and use familiar tools readily at hand.

Divine Assistance is Available

This can never happen when the institution plans and schedules all programs and religious endeavors.

Under such situations, those attending group functions feel they have done God a service, when in reality they have only been an unwilling participant in a scheduled activity. God, the Creator, provides lessons to teach individuals and institutions ways and means to disassemble existing programs and find a solution to the limitations. If there is effort to renew the vision and see the outreach opportunities in the community, Divine assistance is available because God helps those who help themselves. Perhaps spiritual gifts were given to enable believers to enhance their lifestyle witness in the community rather than personal enjoyment. Sadly, many see these spiritual endowments as a function within the worship service and not as equipment for spiritual battles in the real world.

A Spiritual Journey

An official from Ethiopia seeking a closer relationship with God went to Jerusalem to worship and search for ways to improve his spiritual journey. As a Gentile, the Ethiopian was not welcome in the house of worship, but was able to secure a copy of the Scroll of Isaiah as a source of sacred data. Reading this scroll as he journeyed, his spiritual experience changed the outreach mindset. Ethiopia is the oldest independent country in Africa, and the Christian church in Ethiopia owes its existence to the spiritual hunger of this man and the obedience of Philip to move away from a place and become an active person willing to walk in the desert and witness at the first opportunity. Perhaps this is where "Opportunity equals obligation" became a predisposition to act in faith-based witnessing.

The Force Remains at Work

All believers should clearly understand that the force that brought this Ethiopian into the kingdom remains at work; it was not the assembled congregation in Jerusalem, but the obedient walk of a believer that took the Gospel to

one seeking to understand. Obedience to the guidance of
the Spirit will cause a believer to take the right path at the
right time. It appears that God alone adequately prepares
the sinner for conversion, the saint for straightforward
witnessing, creates the situational encounter between saint
and sinner, provides useable material and opens the door
for sharing the good news of redemption.

Need for Disassembling

An instance that illustrates the need for
disassembling the structured outreach agenda happened
when Philip of the Jerusalem church listened to and obeyed
an Angel of the Lord. On a walk in the desert, Philip found
a man seated in a chariot reading the scroll of Isaiah.
He joined himself to the situation and asked, "Do you
understand what you are reading?" The clear answer, "How
can I unless someone explains this to me? Was the prophet
speaking of himself or someone else?" At that time and
place using the same scripture, Philip explained the good
news to the man from Ethiopia. When the stranger from
another culture understood, he believed and requested
initiation through baptism. Philip made sure of his active
faith, baptized a convert and the Ethiopian carried the
Christian message back to his homeland (Acts 8:26-39).
This was not an institutionalized program; it was personal
action at the direction of the Spirit. Such behavior will break
down the over programming and disassemble the structured
outreach and permit individuals to participate in making
disciples.

Individual and Institutional Narrowing

A process called "individual narrowing" occurs in the
lives of most people. As one ages, only enjoyable activities
are continued. Consequently, a narrow view of life develops
and the ability to see broader possibilities is limited. This
limitation is often present in the social groups in which they

participate. As the congregation ages, the same process occurs. With almost no flexibility, the group ends up in a straitjacket of problematic programs that over utilizes the time and energy of the membership and limits outreach to the community. It is up to the younger constituency to disassemble the well-meaning but unworkable programs and introduce a more aggressive outreach initiative based on lifestyle that fulfills the charge of Jesus "As you go make disciples."

Renewal Require Drastic Action

The Psalmist wrote about the renewed youth of eagles (Psalms 103:5). How do eagles renew their youth? An eagle does not die of old age. Normally, an eagle starves to death. What happens is that as an eagle ages there is a secretion from the nostrils that begins to close off their sense of smell. As they lose their ability to smell, they lose their taste and consequently their appetite and desire for food. An old eagle who is in this condition usually uses his last bit of strength to fly to some lofty perch so he can watch the rest of the world go by. He is arrogant and boastful because of memories of hunting and feasting and teaching the young eaglets. The old eagle just sits there and starves to death unless some drastic change occurs to alter his attitude.

Recognize the Problem

Some young eagles recognize the aging problem of the old eagle. The young eagles will fly past him and buzz the old eagle like a fighter pilot. This attempt to shake him loose from the lofty perch usually fails. Then the young eagles fly to the valley, kill a warm bloodied animal, tear a piece of the moist flesh and fly back. As they make close flights past the old eagle with the fresh meat, the young ones eventually get close enough to bump into the old eagle's beak. The juices from the fresh meat dissolve a little of the corrosion and the starving eagle tastes a little of the scent. Hunger begins inside and on the next pass of the young eagle, the old eagle grabs the meat and eats it, and from this gains strength, but the main problem still exists.

Restore Vitality in Outreach

Sensing the need and knowing the answer, the eagle finds a sharp rock. Getting down by the rock and moving his head up and down he hones and sharpens his beak, first on one side and then on the other, until all the corrosion is cleared and a sense of smell regained; now his appetite begins to rage. Back comes his spirit of adventure and the enthusiasm for flying: youth is renewed. He is ready now to rise and take his rightful place in the big wide world. With vision and vitality, he is ready to fly and survey the countryside for opportunities. It was not easy, but the process brought renewal. To restore vitality and enthusiasm to the outreach effort, some hard and specialized work is required.

God uses People

Sacred writings are clear: God used people to advance the mission of grace, not buildings or organized programs. In fact, the message is evident as to the obsolescence of programs and policies related to the Jewish Temple. With the renting of the Temple Veil between the people and the Holy Place at the death of Christ, God opened access to the Holy Place to common folk. Local faith-based congregations must find the ways and means to do the same. Organized religion must again become significant for people: a way for the poor to hear the good news relevant to their circumstance. Why should the community trust the members of a particular congregation who allot funds to property and staff and neglect the underprivileged?

Fortified Edifices

The fortified edifices, with elaborate and costly furnishings, provide little sanctuary for the needy in the community.   The poor, who normally hear the gospel gladly, become alienated through neglect and are outside the sanctuary walls. The ethnic and culturally based sectarian structure of faith-based groups contributes to the cultural stew pot. The little fiefdoms established to protect a particular cultural expression of religion sends the wrong message to the community. A lack of agreement concerning spiritual guidelines and the mixed message contributes to exclusivity; the silent message is one of exclusion. An "us and them" mindset is the subliminal message of the architecture, the programs, and the general behavior of congregations and leads to a form of segregation.

Buildings vs. Lifestyle Witnessing

Organizations are busy constructing buildings rather than fostering a moral lifestyle among constituents. Buildings, not personal witnessing, have become the most planned part of religion, especially, in a society characterized by mobility. Similar structures have replaced many common aspects of personal involvement. The large investment of funds in single use property has become the greatest detriment to the progress of Christianity. Deserted church buildings point to a former presence and the departure of a constituency. These buildings send a message of paradise lost and breed contempt for the pristine faith. Establishing the message of faith in people, rather than property, should be the priority. The objective ought to be confidently assisting individuals in establishing lifestyle witnessing, but construction of buildings continue in the midst of neglected people.

Shaped by Heritage and Culture

Regardless of the background of the people, the forms of worship and the serviceable use of the space shaped the religious buildings. The fastest growing groups, such as the community churches have built modern buildings and are attracting people of the communities who seek to be free from past traditions. Such congregations often down play their sectarian identity with a more generic approach to both building and worship. Yet, the buildings still play a major role in their operation. The personal outreach by the membership remains low or nonexistent.

A Community of Faith

Most faith-based groups consider themselves a community of faith and required people to convene for worship and instruction with little encouragement toward personal devotions. Although there were some aspects of this, the New Testament operated primarily in "house churches" and evangelism was on the roadside and in the marketplace. Sadly, this aspect of religion opened the door for unorthodox and fraudulent teachers to adulterate and prostitute the message of grace. Much of the writing in the New Testament is dealing with false teachers and guidance for newly converted believers scattered without adequate guidance and fellowship. Faith-based groups overcompensated for this difficulty by constructing buildings and requiring regular attendance.

Message of Grace

Although the pristine message of grace was in rural Galilee, the communication of faith flourished in the cities where the people gathered. Faith spread from Jerusalem to Rome along the trade routes, from one city to another. The poor heard the message gladly on the main roads, side streets, and in the marketplace. Converts were vagabonds, migrants, slaves, and traveling merchants. The early faith-based believers were not dependent on a single place of worship; they had a faith received from scattered believers witnessing to their faith as they journeyed. They were often uprooted people, the wandering masses without permanent homes. Jesus claimed to be one without a place to lay His head illustrates the migrant nature of the times. The advancement of faith did not depend on buildings or organized programs; it was dependent on believers actively sharing the story of personal forgiveness and newly found hope for a better life. Faith still exists in a mobile society among individuals who migrate from job to job and community to community searching for a better way forward for their family. Everyone deserves to hear the message of grace.

Witnessing on the Way to Death Row

A letter came from a Texas Death Row inmate Steve Moran requesting books to read. Since the graduate library did not loan books, some personal volumes were sent to him and a friend in North Carolina sent a box of books. Later my son, Barton, wrote a book about Steve and his amazing conversion, and I learned that he had killed several women in Texas and was under multiple death sentences. Despite this criminal past, Steve was hungry to learn all he could about the Christian faith. He wanted to make up for wasted time. I sent him a reading/study plan developed for my students called the Zeta Method for Self-study to guide his reading and making a "learning log."

A Profound Statement

Later Steve wrote to informed me the date had been set for his execution and that he would not appeal since he was guilty. He returned the books together with a summary/ analysis of what he had read since being on Death Row. It was impressive. He assured me that he had read all of them and that many of the men on death row read the books. He asked to keep one book, a modern version of *The Pilgrim's Progress*, for others to read. He assured me the Prison Chaplain would return it. At the close of the last letter, Steve thanked me again for my kindness, and expressed good thoughts for the work of the graduate school I had initiated. Steve closed by saying, "In a few days I will meet God, but I will not die as other men, I have salvation. They will take my life for crimes committed, but my soul is safe." The letter ended with a profound statement, "When I see God, I will tell him about you."

A Significant Victory

Steve Moran died by lethal injection without knowing that Barton, who was writing a book about his life, was my son. We never thought to tell him. Perhaps it was not an issue. Due to some legal conflicts with the secondary people of the story, Barton's book, *Hostage from Heaven*, about the life and conversion of Steve Moran was not published. Sadly, legal stuff hindered the publication of the story. The message of the woman who brought about this conversion remains untold. It was a significant victory for personal witnessing in the twentieth century. The facts of Steve's conversion and his efforts to read and learn all he could would be a source of encouragement to many. He crammed for his final exam. I am confident he received a good grade from the Master Teacher.

New Wine and New Patches

The problem of new wine in old bottles is evident in the faith-based community. The cultural mix creates a confluence of cultures yet buildings are static and send mixed signals. Unlike most religions of the world, non-Catholic congregations outgrow a building, or because of the changing cultural and ethnic mix in the community, the flock relocates. In such cases, a new group often with a different theological persuasion purchases the building and opens a place of worship. The new congregation often has tradition that differs from the previous occupants. When the stately and traditional building has a new or radically different format for worship, the community is confused. Perhaps it is a case of a new patch on an old garment or new wine in old bottles. Three Gospel writers (Mark, Matthew, and Luke) cover the problem of wineskins, but Mark added data about a new patch on an old garment.

21. No one sows a patch of new cloth on an old garment: else the new patch will tear away from the old and the split is made worse. 22. And no one pours new wine into old wineskins: else the new wine will rupture the old wineskins, and the wine and the skins are lost: but new wine must be put into fresh wineskins. (Mark 2:21,22 EDNT)

Mobility and Migration

The mobility of society and immigration since World War II has created a migration and cultural/religious mixture not known before. Refugees from foreign wars settling in various parts of the country not normally impacted by immigrants have changed the face of both the region and religion. A mosque here, a temple there, a new congregation in an old line church, or a downtown church building being used for an entirely new purpose, must indeed confuse the community. In addition to movement from other countries, urban dwellers have relocated to the suburbs and rural folk have migrated to urban areas.

Mixed Messages

One wonders how confused the traveling public would be if the Hilton Hotel suddenly became a Marriott Hotel or an Italian Restaurant unexpectedly became a Chinese Restaurant. Since this would be confusing in the franchised hospitality industry, changing names on places of worship would most certainly be confusing to the community. For example, a mainline Presbyterian building is now a Pentecostal church or an intercity Methodist moves to the suburbs and an Independent Baptist group purchases the property. The changes send a mixed message to the community.

Clues to Identity

Buildings provide clues to the identity of the people who attend worship. The style and location of buildings encroach on the nature of the message. As a group of individuals send to a community a message about their faith, the building becomes a silent message and often invalidates the witness of the congregation. One does not need to be an architect or even a believer to recognize a mosque, a temple, a Catholic Church or a Protestant building.

One can usually identify various groups by the architecture. Baptist churches look different from Methodist churches. Anglican and Lutheran edifices may be similar on the outside, but they are different on the inside. A Presbyterian Church is normally architecturally different from a Baptist building. The shape, size, and the symbols that decorate the buildings usually identify the sectarian group. Even the paint color on the door sends a message: some are red, while others are blue, brown, gray, orange or green. Each color identifies a sectarian group.

Faith-based buildings have recognizable identity because they are part of the cultural inheritance of a community or the ethnic tradition and limitation of a group. Even when buildings are new, certain traditions enables one to recognize a familiarity and associate a building with a particular culture or form of worship. It is obvious that sectarian groups are not dissolving into a homogeneous melting pot and becoming harmonized and standardized pursuing a common faith-based agenda. These are exaggerated claims that should expose a myth; however, many believe that building size matters in the field of religion.

CHAPTER ELEVEN

ABANDON
THE GIANT PARADIGM

Seeing a pregnant woman cleaning the parsonage, my spirit was troubled and Maria was asked, "Why are you here? Why did you leave your husband and four small children and come to America pregnant?" Her humble response shocked me! Maria said in broken English, "In my village the Catholics have a large building and the people think their God is bigger than the God of our small assembly. I came to make money to buy lumber for my husband to build on to our church so people would see our God as being bigger." This happened in 1962. I was astonished that people would compare the size of a building to the size of God or His blessing. At first, I considered this evaluation to be the mindset of a small Third World country; however, in the intervening decades, this attitude has taken hold. The square feet of a building does not determine the size of God!

The Size of a Church

Speaking at a Canadian Church Growth Conference created a discussion about the size of a church. In reviewing my philosophy of church growth, someone suggested that my view depreciated the super-church in favor of the small community congregation. The question was, "How big should a church be?" My response was, "How large should a cow be?" The questioner responded that he did not know. The group decided they should observe and count some cows to determine the average or normal size. The apparent answer was that most mature cows were about the same size. Faith-based groups must abandon the idea that bigger is better.

The Super-sized Congregation

The next question was "What if you owned a cattle ranch and discovered a cow in the pasture that was 25 times larger than all the other cows, what would you do?" A participant answered, "I would get it out of the pasture as quickly as possible before it stepped on the other cows." The case is the same for the super-church. If not in the process of becoming an abnormally large gathering, then soon after – the trampling of other smaller groups in the area begins. This fact exists. Research demonstrated that in one southern city a large Baptist church had brought about the demise of thirteen other small Baptistic congregations. It is the law of the sea: big fish eat little fish. The application to congregation size was evident.

Fishing and Fishers of Men

Hearing the story about Jesus making Peter a fisher of men, as a young boy my desire to go fishing became compelling. My maternal Grandfather lived in an old hotel near the Hiwassee River. The river was normally clear and shallow and I wanted to catch a fish, but I had never been fishing. My father was dead, and I had no big brother to teach me how to fish. There was no one willing to go to the river with me or help me make a fishing pole. I made a big fuss about the whole matter. Finally, my Aunt Lena decided to humor me. She bent a straight pin into a crude fish hook and bent the top of the pin over and tied a string about twelve feet long to the pin and attached it to a garden bean pole.

Aunt Lena walked over to the river and found a safe spot near a shallow place. and told me to put the hook in the water and be quiet. To make matters worse, she warned me that I did not have a fishing license, and if the Game Warden caught me fishing I might go to jail. She left with another warning not to go near the water. "You can't catch a fish if they can see you!"

Fish were swimming in the shallow water, but none would take my bait. I decided to put my hook in front of the fish and jerk. This I did several times, but caught nothing. At last, I was lucky. I snagged a fish in the tail and brought it to the bank. As I landed the fish, I saw a man walking on the railroad bridge that crossed the river. I just knew it was the Game Warden and that my goose was cooked. Running across the plowed field dragging the poor fish behind me, Aunt Lena was surprised. She decided to celebrate my first catch, and transferred water from a rain barrel into a galvanized tub and turned my fish loose. It swam vigorously.

The man from the bridge came by to chat with Aunt Lena. I was scared to death. I just knew he would take me to jail for catching that puny little fish that was not even big enough to eat. Aunt Lena put a tablecloth over the tub to hide the fish and said, "Nobody here been fishing today." He took the cue and made some remarks about the dangers of the river and that only people with a license could fish. He was just a neighbor, but on that hot summer day, he stopped my fishing cold. I never did get good at fishing. I liked catching, but not fishing or the cleaning part. Fishing took too long, and you had to be still and quiet. That was both the hard and boring part.

Aunt Lena said the fish could not grow in the small tub and he probably missed his family. We took it back to the river and turned it loose where it had room to grow. It probably grew to be a whopper. Every time I see the Hiwassee River, I wonder if my fish is still swimming around down there somewhere. Those were the days when aunts and uncles were part of the family and tried to assist the children during their growing up years. I have good memories of my aunts and uncles on both sides of the family. The growth and nurturing of a family is an essential part of a faith-based lifestyle.

Unbridled or Uncontrolled Growth

Unregulated growth is malignant and disposed to cause harm and a dangerous influence that become progressively worse. A congregation on steroids mimics the secondary characteristics of malignant growth. Unbridled or uncontrolled growth in humans is both invasive and destructive. Unlimited growth is abnormal and considered a source of evil or anguish. Growth without development is not good. Anti-trust laws protect trade and commerce from unlawful monopolies and unbridled growth of one aspect of business. There is no such protection for the church. Faith-based congregations need to understand the risks of growth in quantity without improvement in the quality of fellowship or ministry. Individuals become lost in the crowd and families are absorbed in the programming. It is self-evident that the larger the congregation, the greater the limitation on fellowship and nurture.

Troublesome Observation

The passing of time has reinforced the troublesome observation that super-congregations and popular preachers simply draw from other faith-based groups and in fact weaken the total impact of faith-based community. The super-congregation has not increased the total number of active participants in the area. The attendance may be larger, but the people came from other places of worship.

Some Exceptions

Size and weight are important measurements for the young, but a mature adult would normally not be characterized by size. Of course, there are exceptions. Some athletes have value based on size and/or weight, but there are known health and social problems related to achievement in certain sports. The linebacker on the football team or a heavyweight champion boxer may have a few moments of glory, but these are short lived. Fame and

health are here today and gone tomorrow. Aside from the
monetary rewards, most healthy individuals would not wish
to walk in their shoes or take the risks or the punishment
these athletic achievements require.

Quantity vs. Quality

Many congregations seek quantity rather than
quality. The desire to be the largest often weakens the
effort toward excellence. A faith-based congregation should
be both adequate and effective. Quality and quantity are
mutually exclusive; increase one and decrease the other.
There must be proportional balance between these two
elements to maintain a viable state in any organization. The
dynamic aspect of organizational growth and development
goes through predictable stages. A failure to understand
these phases locks the thinking of a congregation into
fixed attitudes that handicap the effectiveness of the group
function. When attendance is valued by a faith-based
gathering, the small family unit has less significance. The
family unit is the most effective communicator of faith-based
principles and moral lifestyle in society.

Who plants the Seed Corn?

The true growth of the past took place in small
congregations. The super-churches of today are "gathering"
the harvest of seeds planted by the ministers and members
of struggling groups over the years. Apostle Paul clearly
stated his intention to "not preached where Christ was
known and not to build upon another man's foundation"
(Romans 15:20 EDNT) What will happen when the super-
church gobbles up the small churches? Will anyone remain
to plant the "seed corn?" The larger groups usually
upwardly delegates ministry to a paid staff who eat the
seed corn or leave it stored in some holy crib. What about
a future harvest for the super-church to gather? There will
be no future harvest without the primary work of sowing

the seed of the Word of God in the community. This is the ministry of individual witnesses; not the bully pulpit of a super-church.

Lost in the Crowd

Being lost in the crowd becomes an attraction to many members of a super-congregation. This has precipitated a lessening of responsibility and personal commitment. As people move to different churches, those left behind have become discouraged thinking those who moved on have become less faithful. This diminishes the crucial fervor of individuals for evangelism and missions. The overall estrangement from faith-based entities by the population has not changed.   Pristine moral principles are not adequately working within the faith-based movement. Somehow, the movement must get back to the roots that caused the Reformers to embrace certain sure and firm principles and articulate these facts in understandable language.

Growth is Temporary

All phases of growth are temporary; consequently, there is no continuous growth.   Understanding this aspect of growth is essential to avoid obstructions to development and adequacy. The constant effort to push quantity causes organized religion to neglect the quality needed to support and strengthen the basic fabric of faith and family.   The striving to build the largest congregation in town or the effort of one local group to attempt the ministry normally left to an organized group with multiple units, brings to mind the dreams of the builders of the Titanic.

Why did the Titanic Sink?

The Titanic's builders wanted to build the largest ship in the world. This was a noble goal, but their ego was larger than the shipbuilding technology of that day. Why did the

Titanic sink? It hit an iceberg--not really. It sank after it hit an iceberg. The Titanic sank quickly because the quality of steel used in construction was unable to withstand the cold. The size of the ship also contributed to the breakup of the steel construction. It sank because the lookout in the crow's nest was alert and signaled the bridge so the ship could turn in an effort to avoid the obstruction. The lookout was correct to warn the bridge. The crew was correct in turning sharply. Had the ship rammed head on into the iceberg it probably would have remained afloat or at least it would have taken longer to sink and many passengers could have survived. By sideswiping the iceberg, the hull was broken, rivets popped, and the fragile steel was unable to withstand the pressure and the freeze factor.

Concept of Brittle Fracture

The steel in the ship was brittle and could not absorb the massive amounts of pressure brought on by the water in the compartments. The ship literally broke apart. The real problem was the high sulfur content of the steel from which the ship was constructed. This made the steel fracture in the cold water under pressure. The steel makers used the best technology available and thought they had done a good job. They did not understand the concept of brittle fracture caused by high sulfur content in the steel. In reality the shipbuilding design and technology was ahead of the knowledge of the steel makers. Those who made the steel were long dead before the technology advanced sufficiently to explain the disaster. The quality of the construction steel in the ship was the reason for the disaster, but the world was not aware of this until eight decades after the ship went to the bottom of the sea. Could the cold formality of worship and the quality of spiritual commitment become the brittle fracture in a large assembly and cause the breakup of some congregations? Perhaps the answer will come decades after a disaster.

Unrealistic Dreams of the Architect

The largest ship of the day, designed to be unsinkable- sank within three hours of hitting the iceberg. Some of the richest men in the world went down with the ship's captain and the architect who designed the unsinkable Titanic. The sinking of the Titanic made changes in shipbuilding, the procedures for handling lifeboats, and in maritime communication. Yet, it was several generations before shipbuilding steel advanced sufficiently to meet the dreams of the architect or the maritime company. Are the supper congregations being built out of wood, hay, and stubble with a foundation on the sand?

Dreams are not Enough

The moral of the Titanic is that dreams or visions may not be adequate for quality construction. It is not sufficient to have a good idea; one must understand the consequences of the idea. Even doing one's job well is not sufficient to avert human loss. The steel makers, the ship builders, or even the alertness of the lookout in the crow's nest or the quick and proper response of the crew on the bridge could not make the difference in the design or the faulty material with which the architect's dreamboat was constructed. It also suggested that the problems of life should be faced head on and the consequences taken. Usually attempts to avert disaster fail because of previous errors in judgment. Building with quality products and people is always a good idea. Perhaps another tragedy is brewing. A wealthy Austrilian is planning to build Titantic II beginning in 2016. Already, individuals are signing up for the maiden voyage. Will people never learn?

Accidents waiting to Happen

Those who plan and develop the structures of religious organizations could learn from the Titanic disaster. Size and money did not make a difference. Many of the plans from the past and the organizations built on the reputation and the good name of previous leaders are simply accidents waiting to happen. The structures of the past do not adequately inform the present. Even religious organizations are made of human design and limited by the human element. Regardless of the spiritual nature of the enterprise, the human factor is still a liability.

Jesus Taught only Twelve

It is an amazing fact that some religious leaders feel they can minister to and shepherd thousands of members on the journey to spiritual fulfillment. Have they forgotten that Jesus Christ Himself consistently taught only twelve, that the early congregations were small house churches filled with the zeal and power of a first generation experience? Jesus actually attempted to cut down the size of His crowd. He saw the crowd as following for the "loaves and fish." On one occasion, only three disciples remained and Jesus told them to go away, too. Peter declared, "Where are we going to go, you have the Words of Life;" consequently, the decision of Peter, James, and John to stay near to the spiritual Source was honored. This was an effort to improve the quality and exactly the opposite of growth in numbers. When considering the quality of moral commitment in the context of this leadership example, it is no wonder so many leaders fail to achieve their lofty goals. Have they forgotten the Book of Numbers is in the Old Testament; perhaps they should be reading the Book of Acts!

Genuine Progress Impeded

Many neglect the anticipatory aspects of growth. Growth causes an institution or organization to become more costly to operate and in the end less effective in many ways. One distinguishing feature characterizing normal developmental growth is the anticipation of future needs, not only for the individual but also for the organization. When planning becomes limited, enough to cut off from view the long-ranged negative consequences of the growth; obstruction of genuine progress will be evident.

Development of a Social Institution

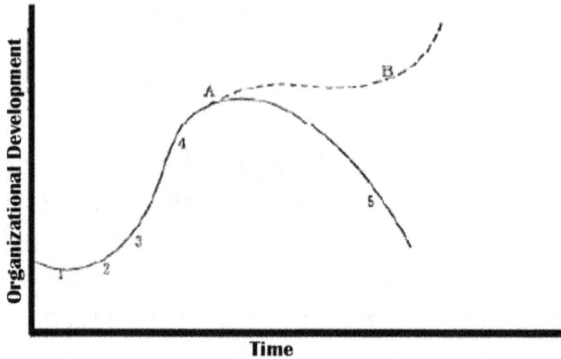

Figure 11.1 Five stages of an organization

In considering the organized church as a "social institution," David O. Moberg determined five stages in the growth and development of an organization. The stages are (1) weak association, (2) formal organization, (3) maximum efficiency (4) institutional stage, and (5) disintegration. These steps seem to suggest an ultimate demoralization of an organization and the ultimate disintegration of an institution. Many decades ago, Findley B. Edge in his quest for vitality in religion wondered if the faith-based groups could stem the tide of institutionalism and the experiential, individual religious experience be preserved within the context of Christianity. This question remains a perplexing dilemma for which faith-based groups have found no solution. Growth will create changes together with some negative consequences. When a group accepts a smaller number than the leader desires, it affects the positional ego and complicates the ministry of presence required to produce effective leadership in a faith-based organization. Equally undesirable are the alternatives.

Blind to Reality

This is not a claim that a religious order or faith-based group must lose the life and dynamics that nurtured it through periods of privation and persecution. Understanding the changes that naturally occur in organizations, leaders will not be blind to the reality that organizations often deteriorate and fail in the fulfillment of their initial mission.   History indicates religious movements such as Judaism, Early Christianity, the Church of the Reformation, and many modern denominations began as vital, dynamic movements, but over time lapsed into cold, lifeless formalism as they matured into institutions. This does not mean that there was no life left in such an organization, it simply means that growth was limited to the resources and the environment in which an organization existed. Yet, the lack of dynamic change and power to meet the needs of society are self-evident.

Maturity and Quality Counts

Growth in size is good for the young, but for the mature size does not count. Value is in development toward maturity and improvement in the quality of life and work. Should the value of faith-based groups be numerical size, the square feet of a facility, or the style of the architecture? What about outcomes and results?   Does the quality of ministry count? Is fruit bearing and harvest important? Does genuine service to society have value?   Does the spiritual value of faith matter?   To determine value or worth by numbers, whether people or funds, is to devalue the worth of faith in society and to demean the sacrificial service of dedicated individuals who have served others without asking for earthly reward.

Worth-ship of God

Worship is a response to the "worth-ship of God" not to the size of the congregation or the nature of the budget.   How much is God worth in the life of an individual or a family? This may not be measurable by scientific means, and may not be self-evident to the public, but it certainly exists.   The basis for value of a faith-based congregation should be the quality of ministry and service to the community, not on attendance, baptisms or budgets. Without an emphasis on the qualitative aspects of development, growth in numbers alone can become a liability. The future impact of faith-based groups on community life will depend more on the quality of the service to people than on meeting attendance or the size of the budget. Faith-based groups must avoid the Titanic blunder. Adjust the vision to include the raw material (people) of the community. Good families construct a spiritual congregation with people of faith. An experiential faith is essential in building an effective faith-based group that can adequately serve a local community.

Lost in a Sea of Faces

No longer does the community congregation exist that was a gathering of family and friends genuinely concerned about the needs of one another. The meeting place has become a gathering where strangers meet in a holy club setting with little concern for the community. Those who gather are lost in the sea of faces and have become spectators without genuine spiritual participation. With declining attendance and half-empty pews, the image of an effective congregation is lost. As faith-based congregations decline, the worthy efforts of missions and evangelism are lost in the sea of forgetfulness. When a group becomes at ease in Zion, the process for positive social change is off course and the people are lost in a sea of faces.

The Pattern of Nature

Organizational growth is not distinct; it follows the pattern of nature. Constructive coordination of differing facets into a complete and cohesive unit gives rise to healthy development in early rapid growth. Growth is not confined to the early stages, but the rate of growth is affected by the developmental phases in which the growth occurs. Some growth may continue as long as there is vitality, but mature growth has more to do with function than with size. Quality and service has meaning in faith-based development.

An organism and an organization continue to grow through cell enlargement and cell duplication. This is part of the maturing and reproductive process and does not always work adequately. In fact, in Miller's Living Systems Theory, the reproductive aspect of a "living system" is the only part of the process that does not have to work to remain viable. A state of growth exists in both an organism and an organization where the unit is alive and well, but may not reproduce. This may explain the lack of the planting of new faith-based groups when a parent group is struggling to maintain their current or existing state of affairs.

The original unit itself may not continue to develop in size. Age retards the aspect of growth that contributes to size, but change continues to be present until death of the organism or the deterioration of the organization. Within this continuity, there are many metamorphosis-like critical periods of discontinued growth. One thing is certain: the process of growth is dynamic and the phases or stages normally relate to the strengthening of the unit rather than to the size.

All growth follows the S-curve normally seen in plant and animal development. The curve also exists in the life of social groups and organizations. The shape of the normal growth curve reveals a similarity between the growth curves of units and the whole. The growth of organized religion and local faith-based congregations follows a similar curve. This growth curve has two opposing forces: a self-accelerating slope and a self-inhibiting slope. A constant rate of growth exists until the available resources both human and material are exhausted. Then following the use of all easily accessible resources, the growth-retarding factors initiate the declining slope.

Nature and Continued Growth

Continued growth is not inherent in nature or the social structure of society. In the wild, one does not normally discover a lion or zebra that has continued to grow much beyond the normal size of the group. Even among domesticated animals, cows in a herd are about the same size and chickens in the barnyard are relatively the same in size and weight. Trees in a forest normally have a fixed size for the area or region. All the corn growing in a field is about the same size and the seed, the soil, and the weather determine this size. A farmer can do little when defective seed, poor soil, or bad weather limits the crop. A similar process exists in the social groups of human society; this includes faith-based congregations. Artificial means does not facilitate true growth in a social unit. Understanding that natural growth is normal and slow will provide leaders the strength not to manipulate growth by artificial means. Spiritual growth is internal and not the result of an external stimulus.

Natural Nourishing

Nature nourishes trees with a supply of a watery liquid called sap. It moves upward in part through an intricate supply system of decreasing pressure. The taller a tree grows the more difficult the natural nourishing becomes. Even a vacuum pump is limited to pulling water higher than about 36 feet. Sap-lifting forces utilize evaporation and transpiration to sustain trees that are taller than normal and not adequately supplied by sap from the root. This is a kind of breathing water through the leaves. In addition, adhesion and cohesion due to the stickiness of molecules in the fluid-carrying vessels nourish growth. It is complicated. The basic rise of the watery fluid is rapid; however, the other nourishing processes are much slower. The larger the tree the more difficult is the nourishing process. This is notably true of fruit-bearing trees. The same is true of a faith-based group that is a tree of life growing in the wilderness of evil. The larger they grow the harder to receive nourishment from the root source.

Areas of Growth

A tree grows in the roots (supply system), just beneath the bark (support system), and at the terminal bud at the end of the limbs (foliage and fruit-bearing system). The constant pruning of fruit trees keeps them within the natural size to receive nourishment from the root system. The church must be aware of the complications of size. This could be the reason smaller groups bear more fruit than the larger ones. Research has demonstrated the viability of the personal witness through a small group to produce converts when compared with the staff oriented program of a larger congregation. Size does affect fruit bearing. There may be foliage, the appearance of life and the promise of fruit, but fruit is limited. Faith-based groups should learn that leaves alone are not sufficient there must be fruit. Jesus cursed the fig tree that had leaves, the evidence of life, but no fruit, the reason for life. What are the implications of this for faith-based groups?

Limits to Size

In plant and animal life, there are limits to natural size. Wood fiber alone could support the growth of a tree up to about 400 feet. The giant redwood trees of California stand high above all other trees on the planet, but they have not reached the limitation of 400 feet (397'4"). The largest wooden church is Austria's Church of the Holy Archangels build in 1776; it is 236 feet tall. Even with prefabricated building modules using wood and concrete, the new Life Cycle Tower in Austria will be only 30 stories or about 310 feet. Using natural material there is always limitation in support of size. When considering a faith-based group built on relationships, the formula [R=n(n-1)]clearly shows the limitations. The number of interpersonal relationships determined by the formula: n=number of people; X (times) the number; minus one. A group of ten (10) people has 10 x 9 or 90 interpersonal relationships. In a congregation of five hundred (500), there are [500 x 499 = 249,500] interpersonal relationships. These limitations include the size of a spiritual group built out of people as stones in the spiritual temple. (1 Peter 2:5). The problem of growth in faith-based groups is self-evident.

The dinosaurs were of enormous size but they are now extinct. Speculation is that the climate changed and food became limited; consequently, the dinosaurs are gone and are relics of a bygone age. Reconstructed dinosaurs made from bone fragments are in museums. Scientist can determine the size and structure and determine the normal size of the animal from the skeletal remains. The limits of environment and structure are obvious and applicable to social organizations. How will the remains of faith-based entities be viewed in the future? Will future generations understand why many failed in their mission?

The Changing Habitat

Determining initial growth rate is by assessing the carrying capacity of the social habitat. The rate of growth decreases and normally leads to an organization of a fixed size. If the social habitat is lost, changed or drastically altered, the organization decreases in proportion to the decrease in the carrying capacity. Despite the limitations of environment, provided an organization can adjust to the changing habitat it may survive, even stabilize and become fixed in size. The fixed size may be considerably smaller than its true potential had the resources and habitat been unlimited. An example is the Swedish Baptist Church that began to die because the number of available Swedes declined. A name change and a mission to reach a larger population were effective in extending the life and effectiveness of this small faith-based group.

Normal Growth Pattern

In examining the organizations of society, a distinct pattern emerges. A look at the three main phases of a normal growth pattern makes the process of organizational growth easier to understand. There is a period of preparation for growth sometimes called the "lag phase." The time of actual growth is called the exponential or logarithmic phase and climaxes in maximum efficiency. This phase usually gives way to healthy development. A constructive coordination of differing facets of the organization creates a uniform whole during this phase.

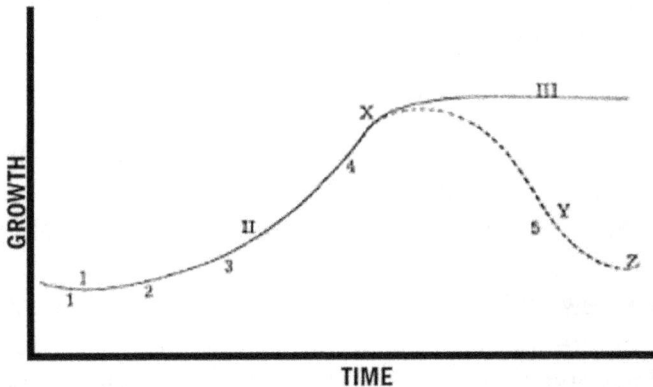

Figure 11.2 - Diagram of the normal growth curve of an organization: I-lag phase, II logarithmic phase, III-stationary phase, x-point of crisis. Y-decreased interest. Z-fixed attitutde that hinders development. Numbers 1-5 are the same in Figure 11.1.

When normal development has reached the extent of resources or environment, a stationary or institutional phase usually develops because of the efforts of the organization to survive. It appears that the synthesized elements used in growth now protect the organization and maintain the existing state. This is why so many faith-based groups ultimately remain about the same size over time when they transition to the institutional stage.

A Turning Point

The transition to the institutional phase is a turning point for the organization and can become a terminal phase. During this critical phase of development, the organization loses its flexibility and operations settle down to routine and often reactionary activities. This defining moment is overcome by channeling the energies and resources previously used for growth and expansion into the creation of institutional structures designed to maintain the *status quo*. Leaders began to concentrate on programs and projects that reflect their personalities and simulate progress or camouflage decline.

A Leveling Off Period

This final phase is a leveling off period when growth ceases and the size stabilizes. In secular organizations this usually calls for mergers, name changes, diversification, or some campaign to influence the public that their product or service is new and improved and therefore better or best, or at least different and consequently better. The application to religious organizations or faith-based congregations is apparent.

Rules are Increasingly Imposed

Developmental growth creates both formal and informal rules. The formal features of the organization are a command and task structure while friendship and interest dominate the informal aspects of the process. The structure changes and modifies the processes operating within the organization as it evolves into an institution. If the organization survives entrance into the institutional stage, formal rules become part of the membership requirement that become less than voluntary. Such rules further strain the organization as institutionalization takes hold.

Institutionalization

Institutionalization is a deliberate process to control the behavior of people. Institutionalization is to be committed to a mental hospital, prison or become acculturated to the culture of a particular organization. Spending a long period in such places deprives the individual of independence and personal responsibility. This may be unintended consequences of such a life, but most institutionalized persons cannot adequately function on the outside and may become psychologically dependent or damaged. Could the institutional syndrome explain why so many members of faith-based groups function only within the group and have little association with the outside world? Could this be why evangelization of the world is not working? Could this condition be the cause of limited outreach of the faith-based groups?

A Kind of Ecclesiastical Franchise

The present institutionalization of the faith-based groups has become a kind of ecclesiastical franchise with quality control inspectors to assure conformity to the protocols of sameness. To be an authentic member of the franchise, there is a required observation of a certain code of conduct, a particular form for sacraments and religious ritual, and specific ecclesiastical etiquette. The process imposes cultural barriers on people when only one thing separates man from God: unbelief that results in disobedience. Yet variations in culture and custom can alienate both individuals and whole groups from a local house of worship. Whether it is behavior, music, food, clothing, or general atmosphere, if it were not in keeping with the newcomer's basic culture, the local faith-based groups become less attractive. In fact, newcomers control the amount of change they accept while holding on to their basic culture.

A Vicious Cycle

Rigid administration of both procedure and process tends to increase efficiency for a time, but ultimately, it produces a vicious cycle that impairs the effectiveness of the organization. Unless there is a relaxation of the formal aspects and an increase of the informal facets, the organization may collapse. The most favorable scenario would be the organization finds a size and continues for a time to be relatively effective with a limited audience. The long-term projection is not good.

Unnecessary Competition

Cooperation and interdependency are necessary in all areas of the faith-based community. Growth in numbers, without consideration of the effect on quality, limits real progress in the development. In spite of the obstacles to quality, faith-based congregations seem determined to increase size and budget without an adequate agenda for using either. This breeds unnecessary competition and personal strife among people and frustrates the whole function of the organization for the benefit of the community. There must be a better way.

Criteria other than the Word

Perhaps a reminder that to serve an organization in the role of administrator is "to serve" the needs of the constituency, it does not mean, "to grow" unless the needs of present members can be met within the context of growth. Since there seems to be no adequate way to measure quality of spirituality or services, an assessment of religiosity becomes a substitute measurement. This means counting noses and nickels and concentrating on budgets and buffets. Each organization can create its own criteria for being religious and project the belief that compliance with the formal aspects of this criteria makes one better than someone who is following another pattern of participation.

Use the Master's Standard

In the field of carpentry, the rule is to measure twice and cut once. If one were to cut a board and then measure the next board by the cut one, the two boards would be uneven. To make certain the same precise measurement, one must always go by the standard of original measurement. The same is true in the development of a photograph. In the old system, one would take a picture and use the negative to print a photograph. Making a negative from the original picture and then producting another photograph, there would a slight deterioration in the quality. Repeating this process and making a new negative and then an additional photo, there is further deterioration in quality. This change in quality shows up on the family tree. When children do not follow the lifestyle and moral standard of parents and grandparents, there is a drastic change in behavior and influence. One must have an external standard by which to judge their behaior.

According to Paul's words, measuring by any criteria other than the Word of God is not wise.

> *12. For we do not have the boldness to compare ourselves with some who approve themselves: but they measuring themselves by their own yardstick, and comparing themselves within their own little circle, do not make sense. 13. We will not measure ourselves beyond the criteria distributed to us by God, a calculation that reaches even to you. (2 Corinthians 10:12-13 EDNT)*

The Loss of Value

The perpetual renewal of the whole structure is imperative to continue to support growth and development, but the tendency is for this renewal to be at an ever-decreasing rate. This is caused by the deterioration and hardening of the vital structures of growth. The slowing of the process with increasing frequency of decay in various functions and facilities reflects this loss of value. The weak personal witness and one-sided praise and worship that produced 300-plus denominations with sectarian leaders, competing agendas, and opposing methodologies needs to be altered for a faith-based lifestyle to be viable for future generations.

Leaders must take the initiative to open the gates to spiritual fellowship and tear down the sectarian walls that hinder renewal and restoration of local congregations. Leaders should reach beyond a narrow heterogeneous congregation, gathered in a stained glass sanctuary, separated from the needs of the people, and remove the spiritual walls that divide a multicultural community where the melting pot has become a simmering stew pot.

Reality redefined the great dream of a perfect society. Society became either a stagnant cesspool or a steaming social stew pot, depending on the point of view. Some would argue the degradation of the spiritual vision needs both the figure of a cesspool and the metaphor of a stew pot to adequately define the current moral and social situation in the world.

CHAPTER TWELVE

DEBUNK
THE MELTING POT THEORY

The Melting Pot is a figure of speech describing a multicultural society becoming more homogeneous. It was an early concept espoused relative to the assimilation of groups of immigrants from many different countries. However, common sense asserts that cultural differences have value and should be preserved; in fact, it was suggested that the melting pot was indeed a stew pot where cultures remain well-defined. It was projected that the diversity within the stew pot could ultimately produce and nourish a civil society. While each culture remains recognizable and a valued ingredient that seasons the whole community, this hopeful outcome has produced division and passionate partisanship.

Similar Assumption

Early Christianity suffered from a similar assumption that all converts would emerge into one new and common culture. Yet, the New Testament record is clear that each community produced a brand of religion particular to their culture. This was further impacted by elements of tradition and ethnicity that included a moral code and ethics. Gradually these elements became part of political and religious thought and are presently expressed in excessive devotion to a party or a particular system of belief. This is where philosophy and theology combine to express ideas and value in a personal ideology.

Moral Deterioration

All citizens must be on guard against moral deterioration that ultimately blocks all constructive change.

The process of integration however is designed to make whole or new by adding or bringing together different parts. The study of theology and/or philosophy creates ones value system and ideology. At the ideas and values level, different individuals and divergent groups find common ground to effect positive social change. This formation is in the affective domain where ideas and values of an individual or groups are derived exclusively through feelings.

Tainted by Moral Deficiencies

In the process of social change there is concern that one does not become tainted by the moral deficiencies of another culture. It is in this regard that one must be vigilant, willing to take a cautious look at other cultures and traditions, but to also be discerning and accept only those aspects that do not violate their moral standard of behavior. The intention is to allow good to overcome evil rather than to sanction the immoral aspects of behavior. Should one accept the dishonorable or dysfunctional aspects of a culture or tradition and begin to imitate negative behavior, a progressive debauchery establishes a slippery slope that produces deterioration and decline in the moral values and meaningful traditions of both the culture and the community.

Location not Theology

In the New Testament each congregation was identified by its location not by theology or a system of beliefs. This difference became a valued distinctive of various groups and produced various brands of Christianity. A group was a specialized entity within a larger religious identity. The brand name identity has further complicated the melting pot; in reality, it literally stirs a simmering stew pot that boils over into society.

Productive Fruit Bearing

The difficulty of integration and productive fruit bearing are illustrated by a red apple tree in my Grandfather's front yard. Curious because one branch produced an apple yellowish in color, he explained that the branch producing the yellow apple was grafted into the red apple tree. It was fascinating to learn how grafting worked.

Taker vs. Giver

With great patience Grandfather explained the grafting process of splitting the branches in a specific way and placing them together. He then showed me about binding them together tightly with twine and covering the whole joint area with bees wax. He shared that the grafting process was limited because the new branch was a "taker" and not a "giver." Nature nourishes trees with a supply of a watery liquid called sap. It moves upward in part through an intricate supply system. It appears the grafted branch sucks nourishment from the roots of the host tree, but it does not give anything back. Other branches assist the tree through sap-lifting forces created by evaporation and transpiration. The grafted branch does not do this breathing of water through the leaves to support the sap-lifting process. The grafted branch uses all the sunshine and rain on its leaves to produce its own yellow apple. It is a strain on the original tree, because the grafted branch actually takes sap away from the other branches bearing red apples. Too many grafts and they would suck the life out of a tree in the process of producing their own fruit. Could this be what has happened in Christianity?

Foliage without Fruit

This philosophy has permeated my adult life and assisted my knowledge of church growth, evangelism, and the development of educational institutions. An understanding of the concept of grafting may clarify the problem as it relates to the integration of communities. One does not have to be a horticulturist to see the disadvantage of foliage without fruit or different kinds of fruit growing on the same tree. Such groups become "takers" without giving a fair share commitment to the infrastructure, which forms the basis for their existence. It's kind of like extended dependence on government; one receives but does not return in taxes.

Givers and Takers

A lesson learned about givers and takers was that most of us at sometime or the other will be on both sides of this question. Takers should work at giving, and givers should not begrudge their giving. Scripture is clear, "It is more blessed to give than to receive." The understanding that a faith-based life was one of giving not taking became clear. Scripture in Romans 11 explains a conceited and egotistical perspective, which resulted in "taking without giving." The character of a grafted branch illustrated the idea. Paul said, "You do not support the root, but the root supports you." A grafted branch does not support the root, which nourishes its life, but the root supports the engrafted branch. The grafted branch may live, grow, produce foliage and even fruit, but remains an unorthodox part of the larger unit. It often becomes militant and radical and is a liability to the original unit. The graft may also become a hindrance to growth and fruit bearing by sapping strength from the source. This may explain the advance of sectarian groups at the expense of basic Christianity. One thing is certain there is no melting pot. Religious expression remains heterogeneous. Religion is not uniform in composition or character, but consists of widely dissimilar elements and parts. There are many walls and partitions that must be broken down to create an integrated and consistent message of grace.

Developmental Growth

My firm belief is that social integration and developmental growth would be much easier if everyone understood the problems related with grafting. An individual or a group cannot long take from the nourishing roots of historic Christianity without giving back their unreserved loyalty and support for the cause of unity in propagating the true message and reality of the historic faith rooted in the New Testament.

Cross-cultural Communication

Without an appreciation for the multicultural stew pot, many unintentionally hinder cross-cultural conversions by failing to realize the complexity of communicating within a different linguistic and cultural framework. Neglecting the study of a second language and failure to value the complexity of culture creates a real barrier to faith-based outreach. The faith-based attitude about cultural and spiritual things is crucial to a winning strategy as the multicultural stew pot boils over into society. An emphasis on difference is to appropriate the value of little changes. Faith-based groups call for conversion, a total change of mind, heart, and lifestyle, without an appreciation of the multicultural environment. There will be an intellectual acceptance of facts without an experiential reality and most things will stay the same.

Change is Difficult

The strength and value of culture makes spiritual regeneration and behavioral change difficult. Faith-based groups must permit God to bring the change. The Divine timetable may be slower than most desire, but forcing change is to deny the deep and abiding hold culture has on the human soul. Spiritual transformation takes time; faith-based groups must be patient and not force the issue. Creation of the Universe took more than a day, neither were the Roman Empire or the British Empire built or torn down in a day.   The progress of social change takes time.

Restricted Message of Grace

There is little difference in the simmering divisions between sectarian groups and the multicultural stew pot. There are mixed messages, exploited motives, deceitful manners, manipulated memories, and dysfunctional members that complicate faith-based outreach. This leads to unworkable programs and a restricted message of grace. Morally and ethically the public sees little difference between faith-based behavior and the action of the general society. This lack of significant appreciation for the multicultural aspects of the community actually hinders the united voice of faith-based groups and weakens any effort to reach the younger generation with the message of grace.

The Great Dream

The newly discovered world was once thought to be the great melting pot where all races, creeds, and cultures could become blended into a pristine commonality. This was called the great dream. One wonders if it were ever a realistic goal. The tactical difference between a dream and a goal is an agenda. No workable plans existed to produce the homogenous community and the melting pot still simmers and boils over into society. The French constructed Statue of Liberty for the world across the Atlantic invited the teaming masses to come to the shores of the new world. They came, but they brought their ethnicity, creeds, culture, and their own dreams. The big dream took a back seat to private aspirations. Everyone was so busy building his or her own private castle in the sky; the great dream turned into a nightmare and suffered a slow and agonizing death. This diminished the hopes and dreams of the population and created more difficulties for the faith-based message of hope and grace.

The Next Generation

Private aspirations relate to individual success or providing better for the next generation. Diplomats and politicians spoke of life, liberty, and the pursuit of happiness, but no agenda was provided to bring everyone aboard the Ark of Liberty. Many were left behind. Some left behind were the guests invited by Miss Liberty. Others were the sick and suffering, homeless and hungry, also those who suffered the wounds of wars were forgotten in the struggle to reach the impossible dream. Those excluded from the marketplace of ideas and work, looked to places of worship for hope and inclusion.

Inclusion is Lost

The true intent of inclusion is lost in the subliminal message of the architecture, the program, and the general atmosphere of the local congregation. Churches produce a stew pot rather than a melting pot. The ethnic and culturally based sectarian structure of faith-based groups contributes to the simmering stew pot. Believers do not demonstrate the central idea that the good news of the gospel is for everyone.

The little kingdoms established to protect a particular cultural expression of faith send the wrong message to the masses. A failure to agree on the ingredients of the message contributes to the mixed feelings and suggests exclusivity for most congregations. The unintended message is one of exclusion. The welcome sign is for only those just like us.

Sanctuary for the Stranger

The faith community should be inclusive. Surely everyone would be welcome in the House of God. Tragically, in the minds of many, the place of worship gradually became a sanctuary for the stranger. The House of Prayer ceased to be a place of worship and became the bully pulpit for expressing sectarian views. The proclamation of sacred truth was neglected until everyone turned a deaf ear to both the message and the messenger. It was as if the congregants were wandering in a wilderness of mixed messages, shady characters, untrustworthy people, unfulfilled promises, broken families, false hopes, and shattered dreams. Unfortunately, many faith-based groups camouflage the decline in participation by advancing changes in buildings, personnel, and programs.

CHAPTER THIRTEEN

STOP CAMOUFLAGING DECLINE

Decline in weekly participation in religious activities is apparent. The lack of converts, the vanishing budget, the public disclosure of clergy immorality, all contribute to public contempt for religion. Not only is there declining participation, most faith-based groups have been unable to maintain even the existing proportion of the increasing population. Children of leaders, families of the faithful and even the poor who historically have gladly listened to the regular proclamation of the good news, are no longer present or have turned a deaf ear to the message. Frequently the poor look to other institutions of secular society to provide for their needs. Efforts to increase funding for basic human needs, such as food and shelter have faltered. The pattern is not the same in all faith-based groups or communities, but the trend exists and is malignant.

Camouflaged Decline

Some disguise declining local participation in terms of a migrating population or changing communities. To make something appear to be something else is to camouflage. The obscuring of decline deceives the public by self-serving explanations; such as, redecorating buildings, adding space, putting up new signs, landscaping, and adding other trappings of prosperity or unnecessary embellishments to attempt to show progress. Some small groups claim the membership has settled to a "despised few" because of the emphasis on quality rather than quantity. Despite the method of concealment or the change in the appurtenances, the influence faith-based group once had on the community is lost. Sponsored events have taken on a civil or social identity rather than being billed as a religious event. These self-serving explanations have camouflaged the trend toward decline. The benefit and power of faith-based groups is slipping away and no one seems to care.

Spiritual Attainment by Attendance

Some local groups developed a philosophy that the group missed something when members were not present, rather than a more positive attitude that the individual missed something by not participating. Faith-based groups have become the only part of organized religion that measures spiritual attainment by the regularity of attendance at religious services. This evaluation of attendance is primarily a modern phenomenon. Most religions attempt to manipulate their followers in some way, but providing a scheme for private behavior, prayers and devotion. Public contempt for the faith-based groups results from this manipulation. The record shows an alarming decline in active participation in the scheduled activities if not the spiritual life of organized religion. This negative participation will not produce a positive outcome for the message of grace.

Participation Out of Tradition

The clearest evidence of decline in participation is in the larger cities, particularly the inner-city areas. Whether the poor abandoned the church or they abandoned the poor is not clear. Those who were previously eager to participate in the spiritual life now depend on drugs, sex and gangs to provide either excitement or a sense of family. The rich and famous, who never depended on the church, continue to ignore religious institutions unless it has some political or a bottom-line value to their career. The community church is no longer a primary source of family cohesiveness or support. Yet, faith-based groups provide many services to the community: baptism, weddings, and funerals, special holiday observances and opportunities to celebrate special family anniversaries. Many participate out of tradition rather than religious fervor. The quantity of the special event participation creates a false sense of life in the church. Although the special events such as baptism, weddings, funerals, Easter and Christmas are important, they do not clearly represent the practical aspects of the message of grace and the faith-based lifestyle.

Traveling Opens Many Doors

Traveling opens many doors for the gospel. The real challenge for a faith-based lifestyle is in the marketplace, out where the people are on a daily basis. At a New York airport waiting in line for a delayed night flight, two gentlemen were in line talking around me. When they would not break line, their conversation was forced on me. Understanding their frustration, my Delta Flying Colonel card was used to take them to a more private place to wait. The Crown Room was almost deserted. Soft drinks were in the refrigerator and little fish crackers on the counter, so the munching began.

Renewal and Commitment

After a while, one asked, "Do you work for the airline?" A negative answer was not sufficient, the follow up question dealt with my occupation. They were told about my travels, writing and speaking. One asked, "What do you write?" Sharing with them about discipleship, evangelism and dying churches, one said, "My church is spiritually dead, and I am too!" With this the other one decided to leave. Alone, God worked His mysterious process of renewal and commitment.

Involvement vs. Attendance

A note on Delta stationary from the Crown Room arrived in the mail. It listed "Seven things God did for me today." Religion is not dead, the cause of Christ is alive and well; it is just functioning better on an individual basis than it is at the organized level. Why is this happening? Faith-based leaders and parents have failed to develop a faith-based culture that includes the practice of personal witness to God's saving grace. Local congregations must seek to enhance the quality of daily involvement by individual believers rather than the quantity of attendance at a religious service.

A Civil Perspective

There are both social and political aspects to forms of religious ceremony and liturgy observed in various communities. Many participate more from a civil perspective than as a religious ceremony. Notwithstanding the failure to see the events as religious, the event actually performs a social role and becomes a stabilizing force in society. Some do not see religion as a part of their personal life, but they see religion playing a social role, dignifying and making an event acceptable or traditional. Those who see or use religions in this manner do not feel a need personally to belong or participate in the regularly scheduled religious activities of a local congregation. Actually, the church and state work together on many issues.

Performance more Civil than Religious

When a minister performs a marriage, it cannot be called a relic of the past; however, in the present secular society the process is more civil than religious. The behavior is more that of an adversary than an adherent. The request for a church wedding is more out of tradition than as a spiritual act; it is not necessarily participation in a spiritual event. These outsiders, although not true adherents, want to behave in a moral manner, but without a personal spiritual commitment. They want to bring up their children under the moral influence of religion without making the dedication as a faithful member. When this is permitted, the process becomes more civil and traditional than religious.

Baptizing Converts

Baptism is another ceremony that brings the family together and stresses the personal responsibility of individuals. In some religious groups, water baptism is the public acknowledgment that the individual has accepted the Christian faith. In other cultures and religious groups, baptism is related to the naming of the child and becomes a kind of religious counterpart to the legal registration of the birth. Regardless, the event brings a sense of responsibility to the family, together with those who witness the event.

A Civil Event

The funeral service and the burial provide benefits for both the family and the community. The ceremony of transition and the hope the process instills in life beyond the grave is a stabilizing force for all concerned and a legally regulated disposition of the body. For families who express no interest in religious services, the funeral and other special services are viewed as little more than a civil event.

Religious Values Neglected

In countries where religion has less influence, the state must provide for marriage, birth records, and disposition of the dead. The tragedy here is that many participate in the ceremonies related to birth, marriage and death without a commitment to the religious institution providing the service. It is as if the process is seen as some necessary event mandated by society. Whether one leaves God out of the process or rules God out of the various passages of life, in reality, there is little difference. It seems in the areas where faith-based groups provide the most service to the community; the religious values are neglected or not understood.

Overlap of Religion and Society

There are other events in life where one encounters the overlap of religion and society. In court one may place a hand on the Bible and swear or affirm to tell the whole truth. The U.S. Senate or the Supreme Court opening with prayer by a chaplain speaks to the issue. In addition, the military chaplaincy and its ministry of presence recognize the need for religion in the life and activities of society. Memorial services for the dead of wars or terrorism manifest the need for religion in the life of the population. When a survey showed that 2,400 sailors were members of the Islamic faith, the U.S. Navy appointed its first Muslim Chaplain. This officer was the second Islamic Chaplain in the military. The U.S. Army had already commissioned an Islamic Chaplain. These two appointments demonstrate the lengths even the government will go to provide an indication of order and care for the religious and cultural needs of groups. When the state participates in such decisions, a large body of literature regulates both the process and the participation. In addition, those who receive the services provided by governmental authorities often see the events as civil rather than religious. Little if any advantage is gained by religious institutions. The separation of church and state is so complete in the minds of some that events are considered civil rather than religious.

Stable Marriages an Advantage

Somehow the faith-based groups must go beyond contributing to the civic culture of the community and develop a moral culture in which individuals feel comfortable and at home. Stable marriages are an advantage for society. Developed religious insight into the meaning of the marriage relationship has made the married status of a woman that of a person instead of a link between a man and his children. The laws that regulate marriage and the ceremonies that solemnize them are a social necessity. The laws are required to protect all parties and particularly the children. The state and religion agree that the partnership of one man and one woman should endure and be a haven for both partners and their children. The nature of the ceremony and the legal papers filed with the court confirm this agreement.

Chastity or Monogamous Relationship

Although faith-based groups still have some influence, the organized religion has been unable to bring sufficient strength to the family unit to make a difference. The breakdown of families and the dissolution of marriage are not significantly different between the faith-based community and the general public. Spiritual leaders have not affected the social problems or general morality more than community leaders. The church has no significant impact on sexuality or immorality. In earlier generations, the church could distinguish between fertility and sexuality. Clergy and parents could inspire responsibility in the young together with respect for the procreative powers. Yet, the church has been unable to formalize a process to affirm chastity before marriage or fidelity in a monogamous relationship.

Conspicuously Silent

Primitive societies celebrate the beginning of adulthood and honor fertility as the source of life. Some religions are uninhibited in relating sex and religion. Christianity is conspicuously silent about puberty and the beginnings of sexual activity. Although Christianity celebrates the marriage relationship between one man and one woman, the emphasis is on the legality of the commitment rather than their relationship. Faith-based groups have said little about the sexual union.

Essential Ingredient of Intimacy

The New Testament advised husbands to follow the example of Christ's love for His Church. This became the model for husband-wife relationship. It was not sexual; it was a loving, caring, and intimate relationship. Sexual response was to be the logical outgrowth of a close and intimate relationship and procreation the predetermined outcome. Some see the "one flesh" idea as the consummation of marriage when in reality it is an expression of the results of the physical union: the child. Husband and wife are not kin to one another and the sex act does not make them one person. It is the sharing of the gene pool that produces a child designed to bring a couple into an even closer bond. By misunderstanding the "one flesh" statement, the Biblical concept of "knowing" which constitutes an essential ingredient of intimacy is lost in the process.

Responsibility for Sexual Activity

The doctrine of original sin, unknown in the Old Testament or the Gospels, came into Christianity by the writing of St. Paul and was elaborated upon by St. Augustine. This teaching hindered the development of a faith-based understanding of human sexuality. The sex act was barely redeemed by its procreative powers and then only in the marriage relationship. Christianity has never adequately come to terms with the passion of sexual love and consequently the dawn of sexual awakening is never celebrated as a gift of a loving Creator. These facts have caused religious leaders to overlook, neglect, and utterly fail to teach male-female relationship in the context of scriptural knowledge and intimacy. Civil law has defined prohibited sexual contact as "carnal knowledge," but faith-based groups have failed to teach adequately the intimate relationship that prepares a couple for the responsibility of sexual activity based on a relationship of spiritual knowledge.

Creation introduced Sexuality

Creation introduced sexuality when God made male and female. The New Testament itself does not adequately inform sexuality; it deals with right and wrong relationships. One must look to Genesis to find the remote premise: God created male and female. God created sexual activity to populate the earth and place the intimacy of relationship between male and female on such a high plane knowing one in an intimate way was the ultimate expression of sexual love. It seems that the divine concept of sexual love was to grow out of a loving relationship of mutual consideration for one another and an adequate regard for the procreative power of the act. Without the long-term commitment to one another and ultimately to children and grandchildren, the physical act of sexual love is misused and abused. The concept of platonic love, amorous even sensual but purely spiritual relationship is considered impossible in modern society. It is, however, exactly the intended foundation for marriage - the ability to relate to one another in a wholesome manner and remain sexually pure until the long-term commitment to marriage is realized.

The Object of Adoration

Although Christianity has neglected the physical aspects of the marriage relationship, those religions and cultures which have placed emphasis on sexuality have not been the ones that have uplifted women. The female's fertility not her sexuality ought to be the object of adoration. Unable adequately to express the respect for the fertility, faith-based groups have abandoned the process and left the celebration of both romantic and sexual love to the imagination of secular society. Society does this through many outlets of modern media. Many of these are brought directly into the home via the television, cell phones, and computers connected to the Internet. Free speech has even protected the Internet and made volumes of sexually explicit data available to young and old alike.

Sexual Expression

Secular society cannot get beyond the sexual conquest or triumph over sexual appetite long enough to achieve a meaningful relationship between man and woman. In fact, the process has degenerated into a perpetual adolescence that is implicit in the failure to take responsibility for the procreative power of sexual expression. There has been no maturation in this aspect of the man-woman connection since Medieval times. Part of the problem is that modern faith-based groups cannot see the relationship between faith and behavior.

The Nuclear Family

Many speak of the family as having value for society. There are political and social entities that see the nuclear family as the essential unit of a moral society.   A nuclear family includes two adults and their children. The term "family values" has a variety of meanings and is often used in political debates when a decline in family as a unit in recent history. Normally, those using the term are promoting traditional marriage with opposition to same-sex marriage. This includes opposition to legalized abortion and sex outside of marriage. Values folk also include in their chatter the need to protect children from obscenity and exploitation. Pornography and homosexuality are included in the values conversation. Lots of folk who talk of family values fail to positively support the value of families. Even faith-based organizations program their activities and schedules in a way that separates the family. The family pew and family altar went out with electricity and central heat. Some say there is no authority left in the home, but they are wrong; the children have the authority. In fact, it is possible now for a child to divorce a family.

Abortion vs. Child Neglect

Those who oppose abortion still neglect the children out of wedlock and born to poor families. Support for a stable family is counter-balanced by divorce among church-goers about equal to the rest of society. Some who speak of no sex before marriage tolerate sex outside of marriage. Others require a mate to remain with an immoral partner. Still others expect a mate to tolerate abusive behavior or even child abusers. These seem to pawn off corrupt thinking for personal gain. This depreciates the value of families.

When only one parent is interested in religious matters, the children are further confused. Children often reason, if being a Christian were so great, dad would be interested. In fact, believers having children by unbelieving spouses have produced a kind of contaminated generation. This infection has grown into a social epidemic of dysfunctional families, drugs, gangs, and violence. The intensity of family dysfunction has changed both religion and society. The talk about family values must be stopped and the value of families initiated in faith-based groups.

Dysfunctional Nature of Families

Faith-based groups have not adequately influenced family life. The dysfunctional nature of families within the religious community is about the same as those in the general public. Although this may speak to the deterioration of society, the faith-based community must accept some responsibility for the failure of the family. Do faith-based groups have an obligation to persuade families in the direction they ought to go? Is this not the essence of moral behavior? Faith-based leadership has been aggressively hypocritical in insisting on their devotion to family values but not modeling or teaching the value of families. The religious community has an Achilles heel when it comes to family values. A lack of role models and accountability for failure clearly exists. There is lots of talk about family values, but little effort to value families in real time. Politicians and ministers talk incessantly about family values, but many programs seem to devalue families. This chatter must be discontinued.

CHAPTER FOURTEEN

DISCONTINUE FAMILY VALUES CHATTER

Muhammad Ali, soon after his conversion to Islam, was seated by my friend, Lewis J. Willis, on a flight out of Atlanta. The boxer's conversion had drastically changed his voice so Mr. Willis asked why he made the switch from Christianity to Islam. His response was shocking. "There was no challenge; Islam gave me a way to change the world." Ali was confident in his statement, firm in his conviction, and satisfied with his decision to be more involved in a different kind of faith-based life. He was interested in religion, just not the weak faith-based kind of expressions to which he had been exposed. Who failed Cassias Clay? Was it clergy or family? Was it the neighborhood school or the community? Did someone fail to lead him to a personal experience with Christ? Who missed an opportunity to harness the strong voice of Cassias Clay as a witness for the Christian faith? Even after Ali's conversion to Islam, the faith-based community did not get the powerful message his decision sent to the world.

True Believers Can Change the World

It is firmly believed the Christian faith provides a means to change individuals and the world, but it is not adequately taught in the home or in religious services. True conversion works. Anything less than total transformation is not valid Christianity. True believers can change the world one person and one day at a time. The big question, "How many others will slip through the cracks and become a spokesperson for another religion?" Christianity must compete for the minds, souls and hearts of the young in both the marketplace and the family home to remain viable.

What have you done today to advance the gospel? In your travels do not miss the opportunity to witness to God's saving grace. Family life parents must accept the challenge of bringing up the next generation. "Opportunity equals obligation" is self-evident, but the responsibility of preparing a child for an adult life of faith is easily discharged. However, for this opportunity there will be accountability.

A Drastic Change

Faith-based groups embrace family values, but neglect the value of families. Both faith-based groups and society have failed to adequately influence families. And parents have neglected to lead their children into the Christian way of life. Faith-based worship and family life have become part of the multicultural mess in current society. Parents are one reason the present generation has turned off the mixed message of grace. The hypocritical lifestyles, the blatant immorality, the obvious unhappiness, all express the failure of the family unit. Drastic change in attitude is needed to make a difference.

Families are Building Blocks

Since families are the building blocks of both religion and society, good families made good churches not the other way around. The early church was instructed to choose as leaders good and stable family men. This was before the church got in the business of thinking programs could build families. Faith-based groups become a reflection of the families within their membership. When controversy and friction are present in the home, it complicates the faith-based witness. To make faith viable in the future, there must be a drastic change in the thinking about families and this includes support and guidance for those seeking marriage and those who may be having relationship difficulties in their family.

"I Just Don't Wike it!"

One example is the case of a family that moved to another city and took a young son to visit a local congregation. The child was taken from the parents and placed in a class for beginners and then into an extended service with other children while the parents joined an adult class and the regular worship service. On the way home the young boy said, "I don't wike it, I just don't wike it!" The child wanted to be with his parents and the parents wanted to supervise their child in a new environment. It was a strange place, much like the first day at kindergarten, and was an unnecessary alienation of both child and parents that created negative attitudes toward the new congregation. The impact of this episode was not positive.

Aggressively Hypocritical

The dysfunctional nature of families within the faith-based community is about the same as those in the general public. Although this may speak to the deterioration of civil society, faith-based groups must accept some responsibility for the failure of the family. If faith-based groups do not persuade families in the direction they ought to go, who will? Is this not an obligation of a house of worship? Faith-based groups have been aggressively hypocritical in insisting on family values but not modeling or teaching the value of families. A lack of role models and accountability for failure clearly exists. The present generation has turned off the mixed message of the Sunday morning pulpit. The chatter about family values has not improved the situation.

Pressures that Undermine Families

The faith-based community has not become a family advocate. Family values are high on the list of priorities, but little real action is taken. No one will admit they are against family values, because most citizens are concerned about the pressures in society that undermine many families. Roughly half of all marriages in North American are dissolved, but many more are dysfunctional. The United States has the highest divorce rate in the world. Some marriages do more harm to the parties, including the children, than a divorce, but faith-based groups do little to assist with this difficulty. Faith-based groups do not adequately advance qualities that make strong family units. This neglect has caused many children to become pawns of the court system.

Primary Family Care

God brings children into the world through families. Parents, siblings, and extended family members have great impact on the child.   Parents must never hand over the rearing of children to the state or to the faith-based community. These areas have a place, but primary care must come from the family. Faith-based groups must reevaluate the role of the family both in the religious education of children and in the spiritual experience of a lifestyle conducive to religious development. Families have an impact on the total development of children that far exceeds what could be expected given the size and fragile family organization.

Overwhelming Evidence

Faith-based groups have neglected family life education.   The needs of the family do not have a prominent aspect in the program for parents or the children. There is overwhelming evidence that what happens within the family impacts not only the human development of the persons involved but affects the church as well. Children and parents have no organized voice to speak about their specific needs. Faith-based groups could and should become that voice. The impact of families on individuals, faith-based groups, community, and ultimately the nation has been ignored. Just as the educational system has been preoccupied with curriculum and the teachers union, faith-based groups have concentrated on the doctrine and polity of the past without a realistic concern for the present needs of the children and their parents.

Concentrate on Minor Things

A strong consensus has emerged about the specifics and characteristics of those families who build and assist human and spiritual development versus those different characteristics of families who undermine and destroy the competence and potential of the children. Family life education advanced both by the public education and faith-based groups must concentrate on the process of education that meets the needs of the children, and the contexts in which this education can best be presented. Faith-based groups are particularly equipped to assist in this process, but the faith community continues to concentrate on minor things. It could be said that most major in minors, because they do not wish to be involved in any controversy.

Most Fragile Social Group

Families are the smallest and most fragile social group and are often overlooked or taken for granted by the faith-based community where building attendance has a priority. Research strongly suggests that the impact of the family unit can outweigh the total effort of both public and private education, even if one throws in religious education. Families have considerable impact of most areas of human growth and development. The interest of parents or guardians directly relates to the intellectual development and learning of children in school. Parents and siblings greatly influence the development of social competence and skills. Both mental and physical health has been tied to the family. Most certainly, the principle aspects of moral development, religious beliefs, and the concept of spirituality relate to the family and influence on the children.

Even the economic well-being and personal happiness and satisfaction with life are related to the effectiveness of family relationships. As the families go, so goes the faith-based community and the nation.

Intellectual Development of Children

Research has demonstrated the impact of families on the intellectual development of children from birth through primary and even beyond secondary education. A powerful dynamic that can support learning is evident even at birth. Some research suggests that inborn qualities, those existing at birth but not hereditary, are acquired during fetal development. Evidence exists that some results of mother-child bonding at birth have been evident five years later. The well-bonded mother talks more to the infant during infancy and childhood and it results in higher intelligence as compared with children without satisfactory mother-child bonding experience.

Neglect of Children

The faith-based community must see the parents as the primary teachers of the children. The quality of family involvement in the growth and development of the child limit the public school system and all religious education programs. Understanding this could revolutionize the traditional approach to education as well as the way the faith-based community approaches the education of children. The first three years are crucial in the life of a child; the foundation for later learning depends on this period. Working through the parents is the most effective way and least expensive way to influence children. Parents have the most impact on academic achievement. Normally, parents are eager to receive information and support for their role as their children's first and most important teachers. The parent's social status, educational level or cultural and religious background makes little difference in their appreciation and receptivity to assistance with their parental roles. The neglect of children is about the same across the board.

Parents vs. Educational Achievement

Educational policy or faith-based programming does not normally recognize the family's role in the educational and religious foundations. This is a false assumption: once children start to school, the school becomes a major influence. Families not only make a powerful impact on the way children learn, but the influence of the family actually outweighs that of the school. As early as 1966, the Coleman Report "Equality of Educational Opportunity" authorized as part of the Civil Rights Act of 1964, reported that schools do not overcome social and educational disadvantage. Children arrive at school unequal and leave even more unequal. Coleman found that family background, rather than the school inputs, most strongly accounts for differences in educational achievement. Could this be true also in the realm of spiritual development?

Coleman's Findings Confirmed

Several studies have confirmed Coleman's findings, but little change has taken place in public policy. Faith-based groups have taken even less notice on the value of families in all aspects of education of the children. It is clear that the school or the faith-based community cannot overcome the neglect of children by their families. The family cannot adequately delegate accountability for this responsibility to others. (Borman and Dowling, 2006)

Negative Participation of Teens

Concurrent with the Coleman study, some faith-based leaders began to search for answers related to the negative participation of teens from faith-based worship and activities. It was discovered that some local programs were divisive to family relations and actually hindered the spiritual development of the child. Some suggested that the nursery experience be limited to diaper changing and breast-feeding so those infants could stay with the mother and experience worship. It was evident that children needed more bonding time with the family during worship and it was expected this bonding would strengthen the child's future worship response. This was totally ignored by the faith-based community.

Fetal Development

A natural sense of the good is normally present at birth. Since learning begins in the womb, the moral and religious training of children should begin with the pregnancy. The fetus clearly responds to food the mother eats, to music, to the mood of the mother, and to the external environment in the home. Would the worship and devotional experience of the mother not also influence the fetus during the months of pregnancy? The mother-child bonding at birth and their nearness during the early years of life accelerates learning. Why then do faith-based groups not take advantage of this and program for the child to experience worship in the arms of the mother or the lap of the father?

A Normal and Logical Act

Recently a pastor came to me with a problem. He was having difficulty with a father who insisted on bring his young daughter to the worship service. In spite of encouragement from the minister and others in the congregation to use the nursery, the father refused to leave his daughter with strangers and insisted on holding her on his lap during the worship service. The pastor and the people thought this was a tragic, selfish act by the father, when in reality it was a normal and logical act by a loving father. The father worked six days each week to cover medical expenses of a sick wife. Sunday was the only day he had to bond with his child. The pastor's dilemma: if he insisted on the nursery the father would stay at home, if he did not, the congregation would complain. Has the church lost all sense of family responsibility to children and parents? Does everyone want a child free worship service? If so, what about Christianity as a family faith? Will family life affect the next generation's participation in the faith-based worship?

Almost Total Alienation

As the faith-based groups continues to program for each age group on various days and evenings of the week; the family is further divided. By the time a child completes elementary school and almost total alienation exists. They want, and even demand, separate church programming as teens. This seems to be good on the surface, but down deep it is a form of separation from the principle function of the church: bringing families together and into communion with each other. As the "separate but equal" programming continues, whole generations are lost from places of worship. With the total secularization of public education and the faulty programming of many faith-based groups, it should seem obvious, to even the casual observer, why there are so many dysfunctional families and half-filled sanctuaries. One only has to view a local congregation on any Sunday morning to understand the missing age cohorts. The children are not there. The teens are not there. A few middle aged married folk and some older people remain, but whole generations are away. Is this the result of programmed alienation through the years when an adequate concern for children is missing?

Detrimental Programming

During recent decades, the local effort to baby sit the children and teach worship to children in a separate service has continued to develop. Now, most parents will not attend a worship service without these perks. Yet, this programming is detrimental to the psychological and spiritual development of the child and clear identification with the family and essential aspects of family worship. Since a child learns even in the womb and the early bonding experiences mark them, what must their earliest subconscious memories be of a place of worship? To be left with strangers, in a strange place, to cry for their mothers, is this really what we want the children to remember? What are they expected to learn in an over crowed, under staffed nursery? What do they experience? If the first impression is the most lasting, no wonder the children are ultimately lost to the total worship experience.

Conveniences becoming Expected

This is not to say that places of worship do not need a program to assist new families with children who have never been exposed to worship.   Also, there may be cases where the needs of the parents for a brief period of time out weight the immediate need of the child.   In such cases, a nursery and a beginner program for young children could be useful as a temporary measure.   The problem is when these conveniences become a norm for all children of families attending worship and there is little understanding of the true nature of what takes place. Many believe this programming places barriers to bring children and young people into the full measure of faith. The absence of bonding with the pastoral ministry may have lasting negative impact on their attitude about worship. By the time children reach the teen years they feel the adult worship is for "adults" and is for grandparents, parents and adult visitors and not appropriate for them.

Good Place for Growing Children

Faith-based groups can become a transcending influence on the family through team leadership.   A team approach to local programming is a winning combination when it includes parents in the discussion an agenda that relate to the family. When this concept is advanced in the cauldron of family and church interaction, both entities becomes more stable. It should be remembered that the breakdown of the family increases the problems in the faith-based community and becomes a major hindrance to the worship experience. A starting place would be to clearly understand the qualities that constitute a strong family. When children develop in a family environment where the parents function as mature members of society, families have many of the same characteristics. They are affectionate, communicating, forgiving, humorous, loving, nurturing, sensitive, sharing, supportive, spiritual, and a good place for growing children.

A Constructive Environment

It is primarily the way good families relate to one another and the outside world that creates a constructive environment for children and builds or weakens the individuals and the unit as a whole. Qualities such as the ability to communicate, a wise use of power, a special bond of love between husband and wife, appreciation and support of each other, assists with the maintenance of their religious beliefs. It creates a respect for the spiritual values and distinguishes between families that strengthen or fail to protect their members from the forces that destroy family unity. These are non-material, relationship qualities that both one and two parent families can manifest. This, however, does not mean that faith-based groups can be ambivalent about the value of marriage.

Contrary Views of Marriage

Data does not support the contrary views of marriage. Some say marriage is good for men and bad for women and that the institution promotes inequality.

Violence against women has caused some to postulate that marriage is unsafe. There is strong evidence that marriage benefits both mental and physical health. Research suggests that to be single, widowed, separated or divorced is harmful to physical and mental health. Married individuals report more happiness than the never married. Men and women are about equally dissatisfied or satisfied with their marriage relationship.

A Strong Predictor

More violence exists in *de facto* relationships than in legal unions. The quality of the marriage relationship is the strongest predictor of overall satisfaction in family life. Individuals joined in marriage, normally do better in almost all aspects of life than do unmarried persons. There is less antisocial and socially disruptive behavior among those settled in a good relationship. Where these facts reflect wise selection of well-adjusted persons or some effect of the marital situation is not known, but the faith-based community should more effectively advance the value of families. A good and stable marriage is the best foundation for both religion and society.

A Lack of Men

The willingness of a faith-based group to accept more female leadership grew more out of a lack of men than an effort to advance women. Notwithstanding the actual reasons for opening the door to women, there has developed a kind of feminization of Christianity. This sends the wrong signal to men, who already attend worship in limited numbers. The message, although unintentional, communicates that faith-based groups can get along without men. This is no more the case than it is in the family.

The Message to the Children

Some families survive without a father, but the message to the children is confused as to the role of the father. This complicates ones view of God, as the Heavenly Father. Research demonstrates that one normally attributes the same qualities to God, the Father, as are attributed to a biological father. Evangelism may become complicated when a child grows up without a father. In an inner city project with children, it was necessary to place an emphasis on Jesus as the Big Brother rather than God as a Father. The church must be careful to give women a rightful role in advancing religion, but care must be taken to send the right message to the men and the children. Men are essential to produce children and they are important to the propagation of the message of grace.

An Opportunity to Influence

Many are wary of big government intrusion into families; this gives faith-based groups an opportunity to influence the nature of the family. This has been neglected. A little effort by the faith-based community could influence better decisions by the parents, particularly about both parents working. Many poor families are stable. Other families that have everything are dysfunctional. Faith-based groups could deal more effectively with the problem of greed, materialism, "keeping up with the Jones," and managing the family budget. Many could be adequately assisted with the funds that are wasted on buildings, full-time staff which work only a few hours per week, and elaborate programs for people who do not need them. In fact many of the faith-based programs work to divide the family.

Dysfunctional Behavior

The faith-based community failed to act positively in the matter of family values. There is a lack of role models and accountability for default. Faith-based groups failed to develop the compelling ideas that transcend the scheduled programs. This produces dysfunctional behavior and leads to parents who fail to go beyond the day to day functioning of the family and bring the family members to a conceptual level of spiritual function. Effort must be made to influence the membership to buy into the ideas of morality and fairness. The transcending ideas must be intertwined in the persona of the parents and in the hearts and minds of the children, but first it must be in the leadership. This is the problem. Such leadership has an Achilles heel.

Priesthood of the Family

Lack of support for the traditional male/female marriage has become a problem for both religion and society. The breakdown of the family increases the problems in education and the community, particularly in the area of drugs and crime. What are the attributes that demonstrate the value of families? When the father accepts the priesthood of the family and assumes a sense of ministry, a commitment to serve others, a true binding of a family unit may take place in an atmosphere of faith and security. This is required to raise a family or build a functioning faith-based congregation.

Assist with Spiritual Development

Many mothers work outside the home. This sharp increase from a generation ago is not all related to the needs of the family budget. It is part of the lifestyle changes that have become operational in society. The percentage of working mothers has increased steadily during the past few decades. There is nothing in the current programming of faith-based groups or the structure of the multicultural society that suggests these changes are temporary. The number of mothers working outside the home will probably increase in the future and with this phenomenon the perils for the family will increase proportionally. Tragically, studies find that most of the working women do so because they seek to be independent. All of the woes of the family, however, cannot be attributed to the working mothers. Many families in which both parents work are stable and wholesome places for children to develop. What this means for faith-based groups is that the working mothers provides an opportunity to assist with the spiritual development of the children.

Adequate to the Task

Leadership in the family depends on ones relationship to God and relationship to others. The adequacy of service is not determined by ones financial status, but by ones spiritual commitment. The effectiveness of caring for others does not depend on what one starts with materially, but what one starts with spiritually. Care relates to being adequate to the present task. With God's enablement, men and women called to build families are equipped by God and enabled to utilize the competence to accomplishing the task without loss or waste. Marriage is ordained by God and children are Divine gifts entrusted to custodial care of parents for a brief period. It would be a great asset if families would operate in a way to enhance the functionality of family roles: husband, wife, parent, child, and siblings.

Stages of Family Social Development

There are at least four stages to social development of families. Some call it progress, others see it as advancement, but in reality it is just change. In fact, little or no progress or real change occurs; things are just repackaged. First there is the stage of **excitement**. There is genuine optimism about the present and the future. The swift pace of sociological change dramatically shortens the duration of enthusiasm for any endeavor whether social or spiritual.

Next comes a period of **assimilation.** Understanding and learning proceed at a rapid pace when one is excited. Learning wanes as excitement cools, but during the period of excitement one assimilates a great amount of data, insights and perspectives. As a sponge, one soaks up relevant information. As excitement cools and information overload occurs, **disenchantment** interrupts the progress of assimilation.

As the flaws in partners are observed, disenchantment happens. When changes and behavior do not square with past experience, disenchantment encroaches on the intellectual and spiritual development and begins to lessen the confidence in others. This precipitates an empty feeling and breeds **dissatisfaction** with the *status quo*. This creates an opening for change. Partners began to actively search for alternatives. This ultimately leads to **withdrawal**.

Unless a deliberate and timely effort at renewal takes place "negative participation" begins and withdrawal is not far away. Families require persistent effort and involvement to maintain agreement. Little is accomplished with limited participation. Excitement comes only from deliberate, reflective thought and consistent effort. In fact, no good will come from the limited involvement of one who is already discouraged.

Children a Primary Responsibility

Congregations and families suffer from similar difficulties: poor communication, behavior disorders, outside pressures, loveless relationships, sinful acts, lack of forgiveness, a deficient agenda, and weak commitment to the value of families. The lesson is clear: the community and the family often fight the wrong battles. The battle of Creation vs. evolution is an example of a lost battle when the discussion got to the courts. Whether it was the Scope

Trial of 1925 or the California battle for scientific creation, the good guys lost.   The theory of evolution was just that, a theory in the textbooks, until a few overzealous folk attempted to force their beliefs about scientific creation on the general public. The court won.   Some fight nobly for prayer in the school, when the real problem is a lack of prayer in the home.   Others urgently fight abortion, but neglect to fight for the adequate upbringing and education of those already born. Certainly faith-based groups and the family have legitimate concerns for the unborn, but the primary responsibility must be to the children already in the homes, or in the courts, or with grandma, or on the streets.

Growing a Garden

The family requires sustained, deliberate, reflective thought until the task of nurturing children is complete. A family is similar to the growing of a garden. A garden requires diligent cultivation, careful prayerful planting, saintly patience, and adequate work from the gardener. After man does his part, the garden must be touched by the Hand of God to be fruitful unto harvest. Parents and guardians are helpers in God's Garden and have delegated responsibility for which God will hold them accountable. Actual accountability cannot be transferred to another. Parents are responsible for custodial care for their children; this is a God given responsibility. It should be remembered that there is a "time limit" on the direct and active aspects of this custodial care. Children grow up and become parents in their own right. Family obligations are a grave task.

Families must Regain Priority

The problem of children must not be framed within the educational or religious paradigm of the present policies. Somehow the community acquired precedence over the family. Families must regain their God given priority. A meaningful lifestyle for the family must replace dependence on either public education or faith-based groups to teach morality and ethics to the next generation. Principles and values are taught better by example than by exhortation. A positive attitude must be developed about the next generation. When people begin with a negative attitude about the young, there is little hope for a positive result. Parents must reject faith-based groups and the state as the primary teachers of the young and return to a kind of contemporary house church where family values can be learned in the process of valuing families.

Worth and Value

Children are produced in the context of the family unit. The community must protect the children and faith-based groups must preserve the children, but both must perform their tasks in the context of the family. Children must remain the wards of the parents. When parents are not religious, the effort of faith-based groups must be to reach the entire family with the message of grace. Although scripture suggests that a child may lead a family toward a spiritual goal, it is not often that children with un-churched parents are able to bring the message of grace into the home. The worth and value of the individual, each soul, must be restored to the faith-based community. Parents, with the support of a renewed faith-based conscience and a re-valued educational system must wage an aggressive battle for the next generation, to assure that morality and ethics have value in the future.

Moral Behavior in a Secular Society

There is hope that in an effort to be moral, society will create an atmosphere in which parents, with the assistance of faith-based groups, can grow and prepare the next generation for ethical involvement in the secular society. These parents must be assisted in becoming spiritual leaders in the home. The faith-based community can provide the materials and the guidance for parents to become the principal teachers of morality. Much of this is done by example. Jesus prayed, "Father, I pray not that you take them out of the world, but keep them from the evil." It can be done, but it must be done by parents or guardians who see the value of children in a family environment.

Parents with Tough Love Applications

Families cannot expect much assistance from the state. It is not the responsibility of government to promote family values. When politicians attempt to advance such an agenda, the public sees it not as real concern, but a means to win elections. In the end the preservation of moral families depend on parents and guardians, especially on parents who set a standard for themselves and their children and then enforce this standard with tough love applications and good examples. Faith-based groups can help in developing the men and women who become partners in procreating and the children.

Family must come First

What exists now is a self-contradicting paradigm. This paradox was forced upon the family, by a humanistic educational system that refuses to allow faith-based concepts in the curriculum and over-extended government that neglects the essence of the mission to care for all the people. The family must come first. The educational program and faith-based groups have a place in the development of the child, but it is not primary. The primary responsibility must be the parents and these other institutions ought to assist the parents with their task. Somehow the family must find a place of focus in society. Perhaps one should long for the time of the family room and family table at home, the family car, the family altar, and the family pew at worship where the whole family journeyed together and sat in a designated pew and furnished their own fire. Could the loss of that family fire be an answer to the present uncertainty or perplexity in the husband/wife; parent/child; faith/family relationship?

Rekindle the Home Fire

Somehow the family must rekindle the home fires and bring it to the place of worship and send it to school with the children. Without such a renewal there is little hope for the family or the faith-based lifestyle. The primary mission must be the equipping of families to adequately prepare the next generation for spiritual involvement in society. How does the local congregation work with families and the community to make Christianity work? The simple answer: the faith-based community must develop a family faith supported by a relational theology that is current, clear and relevant to the community. The outdated expressions and theological gobbledygook must be abandoned and replaced by simple words with relevant meanings clearly understood by the people.

The Seeds of Failure

Success normally contains the seeds of failure even in the kitchen. The recipes of a good cook are in demand and passed to family and friends. As distance between the original cook and the recipes increases, the value diminishes. New cooks do not fully understand the directions and the available ingredients are different. The cooked meals from the old receipts are no longer desirable and new cooks begin to make changes to fit the current demand. By this time the nature and quality of the original cooking is gone forever. Time and change creates a condition that retards the process in accordance with the law of diminishing returns. Perhaps evangelism and missions could become "food for thought" again and central to the behavior of believers. Faith-based groups need some spiritual "meals on wheels" to reach the spiritually hungry in the community. Instead, the congregations still serve antiquated meals in the fellowship hall and invites the community, but they do not come. Discarding the old recipes could be a start and replacing them with spiritual meals that are similar but different from the recipes in the old cookbook.

CHAPTER FIFTEEN

ELIMINATE
OLD COOKING RECIPES

A mountain man living alone and tired of eating the same bachelor stew went to the trading post and ordered a cookbook. When the book of recipes arrived, the old man was frustrated because each recipe began with "Take a clean dish." The recipe instructions were confusing and besides he had no clean dishes. When he returned the cookbook, the store clerk recommended a mail order bride. This would be drastic action for a loner, but he was confused, hungry, and lonely. The old recipes made matters worse. Perhaps a wife could cook better stuff than bachelor stew. The rest of the story is in the history of the west.

Cookbook Recipes and Faith-based Groups

How does the cookbook recipes relate to faith-based groups? Simply, each group of faith must start with "clean dishes." This means that the membership of a faith-based group must be "washed clean by the word."(Ephesians 5:26) A true believer with a working faith that makes converts must first see himself as a moral citizen of the world and then a mystical citizen of heaven. This is a complex statement of a simple plan: one must first make friends and then lead those friends toward an understanding of faith. This becomes clear in Paul's letter to Titus who was working in a troubled community on the island of Crete. Paul emphasized a faith that overcame division and gave instructions on how to deal with disagreement and opposition and how sound words could produce godly living.

1. Remind them they must line up under the authority of governments and comply with those in authority, and be willing to do honorable work, 2. they are not to speak injuriously of anyone and avoid quarreling, be gentle and demonstrate a willingness to learn. 3. For we all were once foolish, disobedient, being deceived and serving as slaves to various desires for pleasures, living in hatred and resentment, detestable ourselves, and hating each other. 4. Then the kindness and saving love of God was made manifest to all men, 5. it was not by personal works of righteousness that we did that saved us, but His mercy, with the cleansing power of rebirth, and restoring of the Holy Spirit; 6. which He poured out in abundance on us through Jesus Christ our Savior; 7. that being declared righteous by His grace, we should be made heirs of eternal life through faith and hopeful expectation. (Titus 3:1-7 EDNT)

A Reference Guide from the Past

A cookbook is a reference guide that contains a collection of recipes from the past. When ingredients and equipment changes, things get confusing and a group is in need of a new cook. The tragedy is that a new cooks often change other things until soon the kitchen or the meals are not recognized. People get used to eating the new stuff by permitting their taste buds to adapt to new food. When the old recipes fail to make sense, the cook begins to improvise and add their own ideas to the cooking. Soon no one recognizes the food as new or remembers the old recipes. It is a new day in the kitchen and the cook has won! Could this be what happened to the freeze-frame explanations of sacred scripture in the systematic theology books? When too many wordsmiths attempt to translate and transform historical writings into another language or culture the meaning changes. An old English idiomatic expression, "Too many cooks in the kitchen spoil the broth", clearly points to the difficulty when too many people attempt to perform the same task, the product is usually inferior. This is why the old theological cookbook recipes are not productive in the faith-based kitchen.

Imitators

New cooks are imitators, they learned by watching others. Cookbooks became reminders for those who already knew how to cook. Present day cooks cannot adequately use old cookbooks because they are incomplete. The old books used measurements not presently understood; for example, "butter the size of an egg" and "1 cupful of butter and lard mixed" or "1 tablespoonful of saleratus dissolved in water." Recipes had to be rewritten: saleratus became baking soda and measurements were redefined. A cup of sugar is larger than a cup of butter. Sugar was a level cup full, but measuring butter was in a smaller cup. Measuring yeast by the teacup would indicate liquid yeast because dried yeast was not available until the beginning of the twentieth century. Not knowing these facts, new cooks made many mistakes. Could there be a parallel in this with what happened to the teachings of scripture when faith-based leaders depended on the old writings from another age and time?

Lessons from old Sugar Cookies

Grandmother's sugar cookies made from scratch from an unwritten receipt. This reinforced their value to the family. Regretfully, the specific ingredients and the amounts used by grandmother are not available in the same forms or proportions. Her pinch of this and cup of that must have been different. The baking pan, the wood stove, and the secret pinch of "love" seem to be missing. The present cookies, although enjoyable, just do not taste the same. Perhaps there are lessons for faith-based groups in the unwritten sugar cookie recipe. Change the recipe, use a different stove, when the ingredients are processed, the outcome will be different. It is impossible to reproduce the sugar cookies that grandmother made. How then can we reproduce exactly what the spiritual fathers said and wrote? The answer is go to the Source: the sacred scripture -- "breathed out by God."

Spiritual Heritage

Spiritual heritage is part of the "love" mixture that makes the present society livable, but it will never be the same as the old timers saw it. Since change is inevitable, faith-based groups in each generation must deal with the principles and the heritage from the past, together with, the essential substance of pristine faith to effect individual and positive change. The essential parts must be included, but will require some rearranging and repackaging to meet the needs of a new generation.

In a Present-day Package

Faith-based worship must have a sense of substance to communicate the message of grace. A faith-based group can work in a multicultural society, provided a pinch of "love" and a cup of "discipline" from the grandparents are added to the mixing bowl of faith. Love breaks down the barriers established by the buildings and programming and opens the doors to the larger community. Believers will need more than "sugar cookies", to make faith work in social and philosophical pluralism. God's love, stripped of baggage from the past, can work wonders when mixed with faith and action. The new cultural mix requires the inclusion of all essential elements and vital parts in a present-day package.

A Divided Faith-based Community

The evidence is clear the faith-based community is divided both culturally and hindered by theological tradition. Obviously, these divisions muddle the message, confuses the central idea, and the population either misunderstands or discards the meaning of the message. This does not happen only in Christianity, all the great religions suffer from traditions and culture in one way or another. There is a gap between the teachings and writings of their chief proponent and behavior of the people. It is logical to assume that faith-based people at a particular place of worship often fails to live the message proclaimed by their spiritual Forefathers. Regular practitioners often ignore this gap. This incompatibility with the message of faith is a primary reason for failure in spreading the good news.

> *14. Remind them of these things, solemnly witnessing before God not to fight with words, for they are not useful but bring destruction to the ones hearing. 15. Be eager to present yourself approved to God, a workman unashamed, cutting straight the word of truth. 16. But avoid blasphemous and worthless chatter: for they will cause more disobeying of the word. 17. And their teaching will eat as does gangrene: among them are Hymenaeus and Philetus; 18. who concerning the truth of the resurrection have behaved badly saying the standing up has already come: and cause the downfall of some in the faith. 19. However, the foundation of God stands firm, having this seal, The Lord knows those who are his. And Let everyone who names the Name of the Lord stand clear from unrighteousness. (2 Timothy 2:14-19 EDNT)*

The Past Influences the Present

Faith-based leaders influenced by the past, normally control congregations. Ancient and historical religions have contributed to the function of religion in most of the world. Since local places of worship were the social and administrative units of many communities in the past, immigrants and literature from the past have influenced the present practice of faith and worship.

Sugar Cookies and the Table of Grace

Many who need the gospel do not attend religious services. Even if they did the faith-baked "sugar cookies" made from an old recipe would not sufficiently entice strangers to the worship table. Since this is the case, how shall individuals hear the message of grace? The only answer is the personal witness of individual believers who share their faith through a lifestyle witness every day. Such an event took place in my life one January. Each year near my birthday, there is a personal effort to pray, plan, and think about the coming year. What can be done differently; what can be done better; what can be done new that would advance the message of grace? During this time of meditation, my impression was to travel to New York City.

Using a credit card to purchase a ticket, a flight was boarded which ended at LaGuardia. A limousine to the hotel and a good night's sleep and then perhaps understanding would come as to why God impressed me to travel to New York. In the bed, almost asleep, the telephone rang. The front desk clerk spoke clearly, Dr. Green come to the lobby, PLEASE." Past ministry had put me in seventeen different churches in the city, but no one knew my plans to be in New York. Quickly, putting my pants over my PJ's, the only thought was to follow directions to the lobby. As the elevator door opened, a man dressed only in pants, no shirt, no shoes, holding a wrecking bar in one hand and a pair of scissors in the other, turned and saw me. "I don't want to be saved," he screamed. At that movement, my mission was clear.

Walking up to the man with an outstretched hand, he gave me his weapons and answered the question about his room on the fifth floor. About this time, the New York police came to make an arrest, but the explanation that the hotel had asked me to handle the situation caused the officer to wait. Agreeing that it was bad whiskey and admitting that a night's sleep could change things for him, the police agreed to put a guard outside his door. He went to sleep. Returning to my room on the ninth floor, my heart was pounding. What was God doing? Were there no Christians in New York City willing to reach out to such a person? Must God bring someone all the way from Atlanta to do the work of personal witnessing? My telephone rang again; it was the man. "Are you the gentlemen who helped me downstairs?" With an affirmative answer, he asked for my prayers. Scheduling a wake-up call at 6:30 AM, and a planned meeting in the coffee shop at 7:15 AM, sleep finally came.

The next morning in the coffee shop, I asked the man a simple question about the Bible. "Do you believe this book is the Word of God?" He was unsure, and on follow-up, said he did not know anyone who believed the Bible. Then, as if out of the clear blue, he said, "An old man in Boston a few weeks ago, talked with me about being born again. He believed the Bible! Do you think that born again business would help me?" The door was open; God was working. A simple explanation about believing with the heart and confessing with the mouth was sufficient. It was not a scheduled religious activity; it was a personal witness in the marketplace that God used to change this life. A letter confirming that change came a few days later on a Washington, DC Chamber of Commerce letterhead. God does work in mysterious ways to feed His sheep and perform His work in the world. This usually happens in a field kitchen with part-time cooks.

Early Stages of Human Development

Religion is recognized as important to the early stages of human development: language, conceptual thinking and social organization. As an essential part of early history, religion is left behind during human development. The purposive control advocates in sociology gives an individual responsibility for the choice of direction

in life. The determinist claim man has no choice but
to follow the path that leads to less and less religious
expression in personal and community life. Yet, there is
toughness in religion, regardless of its form of expression.
Religion will persists and continue to be a part of the human
equation. The obvious conclusion is that what continues will
be less organized and more personalized. Is this far from
the early expressions of faith in the New Testament? Could
the progressive decline of the organized religion be part of a
cycle that could bring human beings back to personal faith
and the moral practice of innate ethics? Could the meaning
of religious symbols be embedded, nonverbally because of
this inborn and instinctive understanding?

An Inherent Faith

One would assume from the known facts that faith
was dead in the old Soviet Union. Yet, on the day the USSR
legally died, the former Foreign Minister returned to a house
of worship for baptism and support. Does this point to an
inherent faith although not outwardly practiced was yet alive
and searching for expression. The academic community has
been an arena where it was not popular to express personal
faith or to question when science infringed on faith and
spiritual reality.

In a 1949 high school science text, the explanation
for atomic energy included the phrase "and other God-like
chemicals and actions." It would not be politically correct
for a present public school text to include such a statement.
Custom prohibits the expression of personal faith. Yet,
the fact that it does not appear in print does not deny the
existence of faith in the heart of many. Consequently, one
cannot judge the strength of personal commitment by
current societal standards. One can only make assumptions
based on an evaluation of current faith-based operations.
Private faith and personal spiritual commitment are alive
and well.

An Appetite for Spiritual Food

Some pessimists would say the faith-based lifestyle has no future, but this denies the force of faith and the strength and power of the personal witness. Others observe the decline of religious observance and predict a bleak future for faith-based groups. The secular optimists suggest that the government and civil agencies perform many functions; such as, weddings, funerals, and charity work and there is little demand for religious services. Some claim the decline in participation in religious activities is evidence of a fading need for the spiritual dimension fostered by faith-based groups. However, the real need for faith and hope are as real as the human need for air, food and water. It is affirmed, as long as faith-based believers share the milk of the Word, the meat of the Gospel, and the fruit of the Spirit, the Breath of God will work wonders and there will be hungry takers with an appetite for spiritual food.

Imaginary Appliances

The present religious kitchen contains many imaginary appliances used to prepare current theological nourishment for unsuspected parishioners under the care and jurisdiction of formal religious leadership. These imaginary appliances may appear to be tongue in cheek expressions, but if one reads between the lines they will understand that they exist and are used to adulterate the message of grace by adding ingredients.

- **Beaters** – to make ingredients unrecognizable;
- **Blenders** – to mix and manipulate the message;
- **Choppers** – to lessen the need to chew and digest;
- **Cutlery** – to trim the over religious;
- **Graters** – to refine and oversimplify;
- **Juicers** – to squeeze and dissolve the fruit;
- **Processors** – to facilitate repetitive tasks;

- **Stirrers** –to blend the ingredients;

- **Toasters** – to warm and firm the bread;

- **Ovens** – to bake and serve to unsuspected worshipers who eat heartily until they are filled with a fashionable cuisine.

Holy Television Cafe

A child was born in ancient Israel at the time the Ark of the Covenant was taken away and the child was named *Ichabod* meaning, *"The glory is departed."* (1 Samuel 4:21) A sign over the door of a closed church was "ICHABOD" and appropriate because the glory was departed. Perhaps a secondary sign over the Church Kitchen, "Kitchen Closed – Cook on Strike" would inform the public. One might as well burn the holy cookbooks because all the old church folk are eating fast food specials at the Holy Television Cafe that serves up exotic and newfangled dishes. Oh, I forgot, the Holy Television Cafe has a framed picture of Jesus (in color), a copy of The Last Supper painting, a couple of old church stained-glass windows with images of Saints, and a large framed copy of the Ten Commandments on the wall. The folk who eat there regularly seem to have deep religious feelings. I understand they have specials on Sunday morning and Wednesday evening and serve a form of electronic communion. How could a meeting of family and friends become a gathering of strangers at an electronic feeding trough? Who would have believed it could be so?

CHAPTER SIXTEEN

REMOVE
SYMBOLIC BARRIERS

Words and symbols have both positive and negative impact on religion because they have deep roots in the culture. When words are not understood, recognizable symbols are used to create meaning without words. Symbols also create a nonverbal message and establish the ambiance of a particular environment. All cultures and institutions use symbols to express ideas and values to constituency. Difficulty exists when symbols are used in religion because they create an atmosphere that may be recognized as adoration and reverence rather than genuine worship which is a true feeling of the worth and value of God in all aspects of life.

Purest Form of Religion

Religion in the purest form is free from blemish and clean without contamination of any kind. In scripture, pure religion was free from extraneous matter; it simply expressed concern for morality and the needs of the fatherless and women lacking a husband. There was no need for elaborate buildings, ornate furniture or manmade symbols. Nothing was to distract from the simplicity of the worship and witness. A precise picture of this pure and pristine religion is clear in the Book of James:

> *27. Free from all that would dim the transparency in belief and conduct before God and the Father is this, to go see and relieve the orphans without a father's protection and the women lacking a husband in their distress, and to keep himself untainted with guilt. (James 1:27 EDNT)*

A Reformation Period

An occurrence of this period was the progressive removal of pictures, images, stained glass, candles, fonts and other past traditional aspects of places of worship. When buildings failed to resembled places of worship from the past, the more they were used for worship alone. Later they came up with a rationale for the use of colored glass to make pictures for the windows and gradually added back symbols and images. As the buildings changed, so the people and their worship changed. This also changed the way the community viewed the buildings and their perception of those who attended. This is also true of children and grandchildren who are influenced by the previous generation. Grandparents and parents still have powerful influence on children both good and bad.

Craft of Stained Glass

The craft of stained glass art is a complicated step-by-step process using spooled lead and cut pieces of colored glass to form picturesque designs and religious icons. The designs are of people and specialized symbols. At times the symbols are misunderstood; for example, Anglicans and Catholics us a Crucifix, to represent Jesus on the Cross, while Protestants use an empty cross to express the Resurrection. Many symbols have a kind of double entendre and an unintended ambiguity comes from language with more than one interpretation. Also, when words are translated and symbols transferred from one language, time and cultural to another the meaning changes. For example, the symbol of a "fish" meant one thing to early Christians and something entirely different to the Roman world.

What is a Saint?

Symbols are not all bad, but they mean more to the young because they are normally ignored by adults.

Perhaps the key to pure religion is to become a "saint," but what is a saint? A young boy was asked this question and his answer was surprising, "A Saint is someone the light shines through." Asked for additional information as to how he came up with the answer, "I learned about saints in the morning worship service. You see the stained glass windows had pictures of Saints from the Bible and during worship I noticed the sunlight would shine through the pictures...a saint is someone the light shines through." What he knew about saints was from sunlight and stained glass windows. Each Sunday morning the sun would shine through the pictures of Saints in the stained glass. It was a good definition of a saint and a profound understanding. Does God's light shine through you? The stained glass barrier could easily be broken if worshipers understood that they must go out into the community and let the glory of God's light shine through them. It would be helpful to remember that John, The Baptist was a "burning and shining light."

The Stained Glass Ghetto

Scripture furnishes ample precedent for a personalized persistent involvement in the marketplace rather that an occasional activity in the stained glass ghetto of a religious sanctuary. The Word of God for all people, is often viewed through cultural glasses and the private interpretation differs from group to group. The wearing of cultural clothes associated with religion also confuses the public. The obvious question, "Why does God dress His people so differently?" This has produced a half-filled sanctuary cloistered behind stained glass windows with half-hearted commitment to the basic tenets of faith. A well-rehearse choir sings beautifully, but the community is not there to hear. The pulpit has a "talking head" to whom no one listens, but lapsed time is noted. There must be a person-to-person witness outside the four walls of a sanctuary to break the stained glass barrier that hinders many from receiving the message of grace.

An Eventful Visit to Jamaica

Early in my ministry, a visit to Jamaica was eventful. My host showed me around the island and explained local customs. We attended religious services, visited politicians, saw a few Rastafarians with dreadlocks, heard some peculiar music, and bought a few things at the straw market. Jamaica is a beautiful place full of history, tradition, and different cultures.

A native girl working in the missionary's home served meals, watched after the children and cleaned the house and grounds. One morning she was not present to serve breakfast. The next morning she returned and I commented, "You were missed yesterday." This was obviously not a proper comment from an American to make to a young Jamaican girl. She awkwardly explained that she had gone to the country to visit her mother, but this old Southern boy responded that she had gone to visit a boyfriend. She was shocked and hurt by this assumption and snapped back, "I am a Christian! I do not have a boyfriend!"

After the young lady left the room, my host explained that I had insulted her. At that period in Jamaican history, Christian young people did not date or meet with the opposite sex without parental permission and supervision. My false assumption had accused her of being sexually active. After this experience, I selected my words more carefully when dealing with people in other cultures. It was a lesson learned: words and actions mean different things in various cultures.

The Problem of Race

Growing up in Chattanooga, Tennessee, the problem of race was never a consideration. There were segregated schools and buses, but it was natural for that period of southern history. It was just accepted, but my paternal Grandfather had taught me not to discriminate against people on a basis of color, but to use character, personality, and faith as criteria for acceptance. Grandfather would use his hand to demonstrate what he meant. "Just like the open hand, people are separated on many social issues, but like the closed fist, people are together in times of need." This was good guidance for a growing boy before Civil Rights came along.

As a teenager, my family lived on the edge of the Black community and I associated freely with children my own age. I didn't understand why we could not attend the same school, but mother explained that the City Fathers made rules and drew district lines, and that the district line ran down the middle of our street. It would have been good if such people had stayed the . . . . out of the good community relationships that the children had developed. Remember, prejudice has to be taught, children are not born with such ideas. Prejudice comes from adults usually out of selfishness or stupidity.

During high school, my weekend job was at a grocery store across the city. One Friday without bus fare, I was walking home. It was a long walk of several miles, but my friend, Willie Wise, drove by and picked me up. "Why are you walking man, this is a bad part of town!" Realizing that I would rather ride, he let me out near my home, and handed me bus fare to go to work the next morning. Now that's a good friend!

Character Counts

A kind gesture confirmed Willie as my best friend. He was older and had been in the army. Life had not been easy for him, Willie was black, but he recognized the need of a poor friend. Willie was what my Grandfather called a "giver." The world would be a better place, if there were more wise men like Willie Wise! I learned that color did not matter, it was character, consideration, and courage that counted.

Feelings about Segregation

My experience with Willie Wise made me more conscious of the problem of race. At every opportunity, I expressed my feeling about segregation. Being from the south, a University of Cincinnati professor put me on the debate side against segregation. We won the debate with the argument that Black people were only discriminated against when they sat down. They could stand in line, order food, buy stuff, even stand on the bus up front, but if they sat down everybody else stood up in protest. My solution was to put stand up desks in the schools, take all the seats out of public transportation and make everyone stand, take the benches out of public parks and places of worship (at that period even the churches were segregated). I used an idea from the Bible that the rulers sat in the gates of the cities and the king had a throne. The seat of authority was the symbol of power; such as, a seat on the Supreme Court. Jesus stood up to read the Torah in the Temple to illustrate that the authority was in the Word not in the reader.

Dr. King's List

Somehow, the audience was convinced that discrimination was based on an attempt to keep people of color out of positions of authority and that it was more political and cultural, than it was racial. My efforts were noticed by Dr. Martin Luther King, Jr. and just before Dr. King died he composed a list of 200 men most interested in Civil Rights in the South. My name appeared on that list. It has been a source of pride through the years.

Equal Opportunity

My consideration for the Equal Opportunity position at the Pentagon by both Carter and Reagan was based on my Civil Rights work. The actual position was Deputy

Assistant Secretary of Defense for Equal Opportunity and was responsible for protecting minorities, both military and civilian, in relation to the Armed Forces. At that time, about 18 million people were under the Equal Opportunity provisions of the Pentagon. Maj. Gen. Jerry R. Curry, USA, was my primary sponsor, but Senator Bill Brock (R-TN) cleared me politically with the White House. With these things in order, Mr. Nofzinger interviewed me at the Pentagon, showed me an office and introduced several high ranking military officers who worked in the E. O. Division.

Mr. Nofzinger asked me a straight question, "Dr. Green, being a member of the cloth, could you enforce the provisions of Equal Opportunity?" My answer was direct and honest, "I actually don't know. For many years, I have encouraged people to associate freely along the basic concepts of equal opportunity. I honestly don't know how I would handle the 'authority' to force people to comply." With this bit of self-disclosure, I began to revise my interest in the position and told Mr. Nofzinger that I would withdraw and go to Tennessee and start a new graduate school.

White Paper for Reagan

My paper affirming that "Only the Majority can Protect the Minority" was sent to President Reagan. The white paper explained that when a woman had the Pentagon position, she assisted blacks and Hispanics, but was unable to do much for women. The same was true when a Black or Hispanic held the position. They assisted others, but were unable to facilitate the advancement of their own minority. The paper called for the elimination of all lower offices of E. O. positions in the Pentagon and asked that the authority, responsibility and accountability for Equal Opportunity remain at the highest offices where there was power and resources to actually do something. The lower E. O. offices could only agitate and litigate and probably cause more harm than good.

Move to Tennessee

Surprisingly, my ideas were worthy, and many positions were abolished. Equal Rights made good progress when those in authority were held accountable rather that passing the buck to some underling where little was ever accomplished. My move to Tennessee laid the foundation stones of Oxford Graduate School (ACRSS) American Centre for Religion Society Studies.   (www.ogs@edu).

Become as a Little Child

Jesus said, "Except you are converted and become as a little child, you will not enter the kingdom"(Matthew 18:3). It would be great if adults could view life and death in a matter of fact way as a child does. To be spiritual about life and death one should remember that Scripture instructs that one should weep when a child is born (anticipating life's troubles) and rejoice at death, (the ultimate healing and final victory opens the door to eternal life). Why are these concepts so foreign in our culture?

Nanny was getting Old

Mother was getting old and my sister in California kept saying to her family, "I want to move back to Tennessee before mother dies." Some years passed, my sister's grandchildren were born and they received the same message that Nanna Green was getting old and was going to die, so they better hurry and move back to Tennessee. Finally, the day came when they all moved back and came to visit mother. Living alone with no small children around, mother's apartment was filled with little nicks n' knacks setting all around. When the two young great-grandsons began to mess with mother's "stuff," she cautioned them not to break anything. Then one of the little boys said, "Oh, it's alright, you're going to die anyway!" As the family recovered, another boy found mother's pantry. It was a large closet filled with shelves of canned goods that mother kept stocked in case she couldn't go to the store. The great-grandson asked, "Nanna Green, when you die, can I have your store?" Children look to the future and give little thought to death. Perhaps faith-based groups should learn from the children and be prepared for life, death, and eternal life in the hereafter! *"Precious in the sight of the Lord is the death of His saints!"* (Psalms 116:15)

Use of their "Outside Voice"

Since death is a part of life and sacred scripture is clear that all must die and face judgment, faith-based groups must realize that salvation is for the whole world. (Hebrews 9:27-28 EDNT) This simply means that the message of grace must get outside the walls of the sanctuary and reach the whole community. This is required to prepare the human race to face life, death and judgment in a right relationship with God. It is not possible to tear down all the houses of worship, but the stained glass barrier that keeps believers "inside" the building and prevents the use of their "outside voice" must be overcome. This will not happen until believers face their own mortality and become conscious that time is short. They will "go" when they realize that the lost will not "come" to the sanctuary to hear the good news, but the witness must be taken "in living color" to where they are. This should be done at the earliest point in time at the furthest distance from a place of worship. Once individuals are truly converted, they can break the mental barrier and realize the doors to the stained glass sanctuary are open for the edification of all believers.

Cultural and Linguistic Barriers

If the Incarnation and the Upper Room experience taught believers anything, it is clear that individuals should not be required to cross cultural and linguistic barriers to hear the good news of saving grace in their native language. However, the character and social fabric of each culture and society constructs walls that limit personal expressions of faith. A wall restrains entry and exit of a defined area. Walls in the faith-based community must be torn down!

Man-made Barriers

Since the days of Job, God is no longer in the wall making business. The hedge about Job was taken down, and Satan tried Job sorely, but righteous Job was triumphant in the end. Presently, in field of religion, walls are manmade barriers that hinder passage in or out of a system of faith. Such a barricade may be based on culture, tradition, or fabricated theology. Normally, spiritual walls are permanent structures and belief systems that bar access or expression. Mentally, the adherents are in a prison of previous patterns and have limited access to additional data that would inform their personal faith. Open and free access to faith-based information should be the objective of spiritual leaders. Tragically, sectarian positions remain artificial manmade barriers to a devout and ethical lifestyle for many. We must.....*Tear Down These Walls!*

ABOUT THE AUTHOR

Hollis L. Green, ThD, PhD, is a Clergy-Educator with public relations and business credentials and doctorates in theology, education, and philosophy. A Distinguished Professor of Education and Social Change at the graduate level for over three decades, Dr. Green is a Diplomate in the Oxford Society of Scholars, and author of 50+ books and numerous articles. He served six years as a member of the U.S. Senate Business Advisory Board and held certified membership in several public relations societies (RPRC, PRSA, and IPRC). He served pastorates in five states, was a denominational official for 18 years, and traveled to lecture and teach in over 100 countries.

Dr. Green was the founder (1974) of Associated Institutional Developers (AID) Ltd., an international Public Relations and Corporate Consultant Company. He was Vice-President (1974-1979) of Luther Rice Seminary (www.lru.edu), and became the founding President (1981) and Chancellor (1991-2008) of Oxford Graduate School, [www.ogs.edu]. As part of a global outreach, Dr. Green founded OASIS UNIVERSITY (2002) in Trinidad, W. I. [www.oasisedu.org] where he continues to lecture and teach and assist the administration as Chancellor. In 2004, he assisted in establishing Greenleaf Global Educational Foundation in Colorado to advance issues related to the current needs of society.

In addition to his other endeavors, Dr. Green launched Global Educational Advance, Inc. (2007) [www.

gea-books.com] to advance higher education and social change through publishing, curriculum development, instruction, library and learning resources, and global book distribution to advance social change. His books and assisting authors in publishing are a logical outgrowth of a fifty-year ministry through education. He serves the Author/ Publisher Partnership PRESS as Corporate Chair and Co-publisher with his son, Barton. Dr. Green continues to travel, speak, teach, write books and work with authors in publishing.

AFTERWORD

FAITH-BASED LIFESTYLE IN A MULTICULTURAL SOCIETY

Change is the one constant factor of life. Any present defense of the viability of faith-based behavior is to say that the structures of the past are good enough for today and the future. This is certainly not true in any other aspect of life or history. Individuals who frequent a house of worship are people and people change. The sacred faith exists in a society, and societies change. God is "the same, yesterday, today, and forever" (Hebrews 13:8), but the human elements of faith and practice change with each generation. Change is constant. The structure, message and communication of the foundations of faith must change to maintain any semblance of viability in the future. The cultural walls that divide people of faith may weaken, but they will remain and continue to influence their lifestyle.

Reading and Behaving

Being a part of the band of believers requires everyone to follow the rules. When individuals in the faith-based community fail to develop a moral lifestyle, it is disturbing. Even individual failure in this area of responsibility causes the whole community to suffer loss. Normally, a new believer is expected to follow the rules and the spiritual guidance of leaders. An example of such drastic change in behavior comes from my visit to Hong Kong. A new believer's note to his mother in mainland China, "I am now **reading** the Bible and **behaving** it," appears to be a clear demonstration of the radical change that faith can bring to life. With limited guidance, he immediately saw the value of living what he learned from sacred writings. Full commitment to a faith-based existence is supposed to regenerate the soul and redirect the priorities toward a moral lifestyle. Such change also creates a desire to read and heed the words of pristine faith.

New Creation vs. Reincarnation

According to sacred writings, spiritual conversion is to produce a new creation that generates a revitalized lifestyle and brings into being a moral witness. We need more converts who clearly **believe** and **behave** the words of the inspired text. Discussing this issue with a young Hindu in the Caribbean, he was concerned about reincarnation. He asked, "Why does your religion not teach reincarnation?" With an affirmative statement, the difference between reincarnation and new creation was explained. Using (2 Corinthians 5:17, 18b) the explanation was made that my religion dealt with settling the issue of the afterlife before death. Christian converts settle this issue before death and have no uncertainty about eternity. Believers should have assurance not surprises.

> *Therefore, if any man be in Christ, he is a new creation: observe, the old things have passed away; all things have become new. 18. All things are of God, who has brought us together in Himself.... (2 Corinthians 5:17, 18b EDNT).*

Tear Down the Walls

Individuals must become more involved in the process of sharing the message of grace. Personal initiative to break down the walls that divide people of faith must become the norm, not an exception. Faith-based groups seem to be fragmented, stagnant, and unable to communicate a unified message to the public because of the walls that divide people from each other. The gates to these dividing walls must first be opened to free passage and then the walls themselves will begin to crumble so all may clearly see the Right Path to God's grace and forgiveness.

Empty Pulpit

One priest wrote at the middle of the last century *"Most congregations have no chance to express their minds, and so they sleep all through the sermon, lulled by the drone of our voices and by the unreal truisms we are mouthing"* (Michonniau, 1950). The trouble with the church, wrote Doberstein *"preaching itself has decayed and disintegrated to the point where it is close to the stage of dying."* (Doberstein, 1965) Clyde Reid, in his seminal work on preaching as communication, declared the religious pulpit to be empty. *"The pulpit today is empty in the sense that there is often no message heard, no results seen, and no power felt"* (Reid, 1967). During the intervening decades the empty pulpit syndrome has produced half-filled sanctuaries cloistered within four-walls, adorned with stained glass windows and occupied with half-hearted worshipers with little understanding of the basic tenets of the historic faith. The tragedy is compounded by the fact that no one ventures outside the walls to present a message of life-changing faith to the community.

An Unfinished Task

Donald A. McGavran in a Foreword to my book *Why Churches Die,* acknowledged that some groups were declining. *"And this, at a time when less than half the citizens and the youth are practicing Christians. Though the population is expanding, thousands of congregations are smaller now than they were a few years ago."* Dr. McGavran characterizing the condition of worship services then wrote: *"While churches sicken and die, while two billion have not yet heard effectively the name of Jesus Christ, whole denominations spend almost all their resources on things other than disciplining men and women."* The global integration of faith in the lives of common folk who would gladly listen to the good news is the tragic and unfinished task of the faith-based community. (Green 1972, 2007)

An Intrusive Multicultural Society

As faith-based groups progress in the Twenty-first Century, the situation is even worse. The faith-based community has been unable to bridge the great fixed gulf between culture and faith, break down the dividing walls of sectarianism, or reduce the negative effect of an intrusive multicultural society into the life-style of people of faith. Although world leaders have been identified with religion, their "bully pulpit" together with the combined pulpits of thousands of clergy has not prevented the progressive debauchery in the lives of the people. This seems to be worse in some parts of the world than in others. The public involvement in political causes by those who claim faith-based membership has not prevented discrimination, eliminated injustice, fed the hungry, clothed the naked, or ministered to the fatherless and the widows in the world.

Assembled Together in a Spiritual Sanctuary

11. Remember your nature as Gentiles, that you did not physically conform to the Jewish tradition; 12. that you were without Christ, being outside the commonwealth of Israel, and outside the covenants of promise, without hope, and without God in the world: 13. but now in Christ Jesus you who were outside are brought inside the promises by the blood of Christ. 14. For He is the bond of peace that unites both parts into one having dissolved the partition between us; 15. abolishing by His death the hostility, even the law with its decrees and rules; in order to bring together Jew and Gentile into one quality man and produce peace; 16. and unite both in God through His body on the cross, and thereby destroy their mutual hostility: 17. and came and proclaimed peace from hostility to both far and near. 18. For through Him we both have the right of entry to the Father's promises by one Spirit. 19. Therefore you are no more outsiders, but fellow citizens with the saints, and belong to the household of God; 20. and are now built on the foundation of the prophets and the apostles, Jesus Christ Himself being the foundation stone; 21. in whom the whole building is closely joined together and growing into a sacred temple in the Lord: 22. in Christ you are now assembled together in a spiritual sanctuary through the Spirit. (Ephesians 2:11-22 EDNT)

A Generic Blindness

My sixty-year (60) attempt to support religion at a personal and a congregational level required a generic blindness to the sectarian nature of local places of worship and provided a less biased framework for social research related to the barrier walls caused by failure of faith-based behavior. The effort to understand faith-based groups as social institutions and develop an appreciation for religious heritage enhanced my personal spiritual life and provided a basis for continued social scientific research.

Antecedent Causes for Sectarian Divisions

Most faith-based divisions can be traced to cultural roots, national origins or the ego of men. Jude wrote about those who caused separations and divisions because they were men of the world without the Spirit. (Jude 19) My search for causes antecedent to sectarian divisions has taken me into every region of the United States and required extensive travel in forty-six (46) countries. Research was directed toward the social and cultural foundations of sectarian groups. The problem of negative participation in religious worship has created declining attendance, as well as the destructive aspects of personal mental reservation to commitment and blatant disagreement with the tenets of faith. In an effort to understand the sectarian view, extensive research was done on the oldest Pentecostal group and the largest Protestant group. Doctorates in Theology and Philosophy were earned during this search.

Meanwhile, my schedule was filled with academic research and writing, but colleagues and friends have encouraged a sequel to my best known works. *Tear Down These Walls* is an attempt to follow that prompt. Over the years, this research was published in various books:

Hitching your Star to a Wagon (1958) – An effort to guide youth in finding a vocational direction.

Discipleship (1962, 2010) dealt with the individual and the personal Christian witness.

Christian Education Cyclopedia (1965) – Preserving workable programs and methods in church-based education for the next generation of leadership.

Marching As To War (1969) – Recording a denominational history for the benefit of future generations.

Understanding Pentecostalism (1970) – Understanding the effect of a particular doctrine on individual members at the congregational level.

Why Churches Die (1972, 2007) – Assessing congregational vitality to determine thirty-five reasons why congregations were losing their pristine power of outreach.

Why Wait Till Sunday? (1975, 2012) – A renewal plan for weak congregations troubled by the "human factor" and the problem of "upward delegation."

Understanding Scientific Research (1982) – A research text for the social professions in an effort to get others involved in research related to morality and ethics in business and industry, principles and values in the social professions, and the sociological integration of religion and society.

Interpreting an Author's Words (2008) Refine study and writing skills by understanding how to interpret the written words of others.

Titanic Lessons (2008, 2012) – An answer to the question: "Do historic realities predict problems for a growing faith-based group?

Fighting the Amalekites (2008, 2013) -- Spiritual warfare against unhealthy addictions, unproductive habits, an uncontrolled tongue, and the little "Amalekites" that ambush and take advantage of spiritual weaknesses.

Remedial and Surrogate Parenting (2009, 2013) --Children are a gift of God and a legacy of faith-based families; therefore, parenting skills are an essential aspect of religion. This work is guidance for remedial human development (0-20) for parents, teachers, and childcare workers.

Why Christianity Fails in America (2010) -- A call for an internal redirection of the heart and soul to make the pristine faith viable in the Twenty-first century.

How to Build a Better Spouse Trap (2010) -- A major failure of faith-based groups is they have made little difference in the lives of individuals and their function in the family. How to choose a mate, learn for our mistakes, stay married, and teach others to break the cycle of dysfunctional relationships. The family unit is a microcosm of faith-based behavior.

Sympathetic Leadership Cybernetics (2007, 2010) -- Charting a course for organizations to serve the needs of people through shepherd management and servant leadership.

SO TALES (2011) -- Preserving true stories from the past for the benefit of family and friends.

Designing Valid Research (2011) -- Assistance for students in producing compelling social research supported by tested hypotheses.

The EVERGREEN Devotional New Testament -- Complete Edition (2012, 2013) -- EDNT is a 42-year project to translate common NT Greek and determine the meaning "then" and how words can best be expressed "now" and remain true to the original intent expressed in a common devotional language.

Transformational Leadership in Education -Second Edition (2013) -- A strengths-based approach in education for administrators, teachers, and guidance counselors.

Tear Down These Walls (2013) – A priority agenda must be to make people moral citizens of the world before they can become mystical citizens of heaven. Where organized groups choose not to function, personal action could make a difference and break down some of the barriers that divide the faith-based community and strengthen the One Lord-One Faith message.

Research Methods for Problem Solvers and Critical Thinkers (2013) – Guidance for students in tertiary education in the development of a thesis and constructing a dissertation in the social sciences with an objective of positive social change.

[These books may be found at www.gea-books.com/bookstore and at other Internet sites where good books are sold.]

REFERENCE BIBLIOGRAPHY

Anderson, B. (1983). Imagined Communities: Reflections on the Origin and Spread of Nationalism, Verso, London.

Banting, K. and Kymlicka, W. (eds) (2006). Multiculturalism and the Welfare State, Oxford University Press, Oxford.

Bartholomew, W, Craig G. and Goheen, Michael (2002) *Finding Our Place in the Biblical Story*. Grand Rapids: Baker.

Bean, F. and Stevens, G. (2003). *America's Newcomers and the Dynamics of Diversity*, Russell Sage Foundation, New York.

Ben-Rafael, E., Sternberg, Y. , vol.eds. (2010). World Religions and Multiculturalism (A Dialectic Relation) Volume 23, Series: *International Comparative Social Studies*. Brill, Israel.

Blainey, G. (1994). 'Melting Pot on the Boil', *The Bulletin*, 30 August: 22-27.

Bonhoeffer, Dietrich (1937.1966) *The Cost of Discipleship.* New York: Macmillan

Bonhoeffer, Dietrich (1985) *Spiritual Care*. Minneapolis: Fortress Press.

Borman, Geoffrey, and N. Maritza Dowling, (2006) *Schools and Inequality: A Multilevel Analysis of Coleman's Inequality of Educational Opportunity.* Data: (pbaker@wisc.edu)

Borthwick, Paul (2003) *Stop Witnessing and Start Loving.* NavPress

Brubaker, R. (2001) 'The return of assimilation? Changing perspectives on immigration and its sequels in France, Germany, and the United States', *Ethnic and Racial Studies*, vol. 24, 4:531-

Cahill, D., Bouma, G., Dellal, H. and Leahy, M. (2004). *Religion, Cultural Diversity and Safeguarding Australia*, Australian Multicultural Foundation, Melbourne.

Clyne, M. (2003). *Dynamics of Language Contact*, Cambridge University Press, Cambridge.

Dahl, R. A. (1967). *Pluralist democracy in the United States: Conflict and consent*, Rand McNally, Chicago.

Darrell L. Whiteman, "Contextualization: The Theory, the Gap, the Challenge," *International Bulletin of Missionary Research*, January, 1997.

Doberstein, John W. (1965). *Trouble with the Church*, [Translation of Helmut Thielicke by Doberstein] Harper & Row.

Drachsler, J. (1920). Democracy and Assimilation: The Blending of Immigrant Heritages in America, the Macmillan Company, New York.

Dunagin, Richard L. (1999) *Beyond These Walls.* Nashville: Abingdon Press.

Fergusson, D. (2004). *Church, State and Civil Society*, Cambridge University Press.

Fishman, J. A.. (1968). *Readings in the Sociology of Language*, Mouton, The Hague.

Glazer, N. and Moynihan, D. P. (1963). *Beyond the Melting Pot: The Negroes, Puerto Ricans, Jews, Italians, and Irish of New York City*, MIT Press and Harvard University Press, Cambridge, Mass.

Gordon, M. M. (1964). *Assimilation in American Life: The Role of Race, Religion, and National Origins*, Oxford University Press, New York.

Green, Hollis L. (2007) *Discipleship.* Nashville: GlobalEdAdvancePress.

Green, Hollis L. (2007) *Why Christianity Fails in America.* Nashville: GlobalEdAdvancePress.

Green, Hollis L. (2007) *Why Churches Die*, Nashville: GlobalEdAdvancePress.

Green, Hollis L. (2008) *Fighting the Amalekites*. Nashville: GlobalEdAdvancePress.

Green, Hollis L. (2010) *Sympathetic Leadership Cybernetics*. Nashville: GlobalEdAdvancePress.

Green, Hollis L. (2012) *The EVERGREEN Devotional New Testament (Complete Edition)*, Nashville: GlobalEdAdvancePress.

Green, Michael, *ed.* (2002) *Church Without Walls: A Global Examination of the Cell Church*. Grand Rapids: Eerdman.

Gunnell, J. G. (2004). *Imagining the American Polity: Political Science and the Discourses of Heath*, Oxford University Press for the British Academy, Oxford.

Herberg, W. (1955). *Protestant–Catholic–Jew: An Essay in American Religious Sociology*, Doubleday, Garden City, NY.

Hirst, P. (ed) (1989). *The Pluralist Theory of the State*: Selected Writings of G. D. H. Cole, J. N. Figgis and H. J. Laski, Routledge, London.

Hogan, M. (1987). *The Sectarian Strand*, Penguin, Ringwood, Victoria.

Huntington, S. P. (1996). *The Clash of Civilizations and the Remaking of World Order*, Simon and Schuster, New York.

Hybels, Bill. (2006) *Just Walk Across The Room: Simple Steps to Pointing People to Faith*. Grand Rapids: Zondervan.

Jones, Larry (2009) *The Black Church Heritage*. Nashville: GlobalEdAdvancePress.

Kaya, A. (2009). *Islam, Migration and Integration: The Age of Securitization*, Palgrave Macmillan.

Kittell, Theodore H. (2011) *Faith-Based Leadership and Management: How Personal Viewpoints and*

Values Influence an Organization. Nashville: GlobalEdAdvancePress.

Michonniau, Abbe' G. (1950) *Revolution in a City Parish*. Newman Press.

Ramjattan, Subesh (2011) *God's Work Done God's Way*. Nashville: GlobalEdAdvancePress.

Ramjattan, Subesh (2013) *Navigating The Challenges of Faith-Based Behavior*. Nashville: GlobalEdAdvancePress.

Reid, Clyde, (1967) *The Empty Pulpit*. Harper & Row.

Register, Ray G. (2009) *Discipling Middle Eastern Believers*. Nashville: GlobalEdAdvancePress.

Salili, Farideth, Hoosain, Rumjahn,(Eds.) (2003) *Teaching, Learning, and Motivation in a Multicultural Context*. U of Hong Kong.

Salili, Farideth, Hoosain, Rumjahn,(Eds.) (2006) *Research in Multicultural Education and International Perspectives*. U of Hong Kong.

Sardar, Zuhdi (2011). *Between Iraq & Hard Places*. Nashville: GlobalEdAdvancePress.

Somerville, George K. (2013) *The Faith of Christ Jesus: Lost on Planet Earth*. Nashville: GlobalEdAdvancePress.

Zangwill, I (1909). *The Melting-Pot: Drama in Four Acts*, Macmillan, New York

www.ingramcontent.com/pod-product-compliance
Lightning Source LLC
Chambersburg PA
CBHW031251090426
42742CB00007B/399